MW00629097

BADASS
YOUR BRAND

The Impatient Entrepreneur's Guide
to Turning Expertise into Profit

Pia Silva

For information contact;
Worstofall Design LLC
37 Greenpoint Ave
Suite E3B
Brooklyn, NY 11222
www.worstofalldesign.com

ISBN: 978-0-9987143-0-1

First Edition: March 2017
Printed in the United States of America
10 9 8 7 6 5 4 3 2 1

To all the Badass entrepreneurs
who dream of a life doing what
they love, and to my most
inspirational dreamer of all, Steve

CONTENTS

"Too bad, I was really thirsty."

INTRODUCTION

I'm freaking out. Am I going to have to call it quits and get a REAL job? My business partner, Steve, and I are sitting at the kitchen table in our little railroad apartment in Brooklyn. It's been three months since we've closed a single client. Correction: Since *I've* closed a single client.

After three years of hunting for customers for our branding company, Worstofall Design, I hit a breaking point. I was burned out on 5:45 a.m. wake-ups for networking meetings and marathons of coffee dates that were offering no results—with no end in sight. For the first time in my life, I was considering giving up.

We'd had many stressful times before, of course, but this was the first time I was actually *crying* over it. We had $40,000 of credit card debt, and were getting in deeper every month. And now, even if the best-case scenario panned out and some of our pending proposals closed, it wouldn't make much of a dent. I was learning how expensive it is not to have any money—interest fees, late fees, and the like were piling up.

Steve, who also happens to be my husband, suggested we let our two employees go. *Let the employees go?!* NEVER! That was the furthest thing from my mind. We were building something, and letting them go meant admitting defeat. I couldn't accept that I was going to be one of those failed-business statistics at exactly the three-year mark.

Our story isn't one of overcoming immense hardship. Steve and I both grew up with resources and good educations. We knew that even if we failed at this business we would never be hungry or on the street. Our story also isn't about sudden, unfathomable success. We aren't millionaires, and our company didn't blow up like Facebook.

It's about our burning desire to create something from nothing. It's about defining success for ourselves, and our motivation to find success by doing things our way. And it's about the freedom to create and execute our ideas, and then share those ideas with the world. It's about the thing I believe most entrepreneurs today are looking for.

That little meltdown happened on a Friday in March

2014. The following Monday, we let our two employees go, falling (or pushing ourselves) over the proverbial cliff.

But over the nine months that followed, we grew wings. We ended up having our best and most profitable year, with no signs of it letting up. I also stopped networking completely and started taking weekends off. By June 2015, we had made $500,000 in revenue by selling only our services, without paying for advertising, and working for clients a mere three days a week.

I want to share exactly how we did it, and how we have done the same for many successful clients.

It all comes down to two words: BADASS BRAND.

We knew we were drowning on that fateful night in the winter of 2014. Steve suggested we do the one thing that would obviously help us quickly: downsize. I resisted because I thought downsizing meant failure. But when he clarified what he meant, it was one of the most brilliant things I had ever heard him say. He insisted that this wasn't a move backward, but a move forward. We weren't failures. We're good at what we do! We have happy clients who love our work.

But we were clearly failing at something, and that's what we needed to identify and fix. And he said it was time we took our own medicine. He was right.

THE SHOEMAKER'S SON...WEARS LOUBOUTINS

I hear the phrase "the shoemaker's son has no shoes" far too often. It refers to small business owners who are so busy working with clients that they neglect their own business. The worst is when they don't do for their own business the very service they provide to others.

It's the social media company with a paltry social media presence. A web designer with an outdated website. A content writer without a blog.

And I realized at this critical moment that it frustrated me so much because I was doing *the very same thing.*

TAKE YOUR OWN MEDICINE

The most valuable asset we had at the time—and the one most entrepreneurs have—is a deep understanding of our own area of expertise. With no money, we had to leverage what we had, and we realized it was pretty valuable! Our clients—albeit few and far between—were paying us $30,000 for our services, so we must have been doing something right.

So we put ourselves through our own process, and we got staggering results. This led to a complete 180 wherein we transformed our business from struggling to Badass. This book shows you exactly how we took our company from being $40,000 in debt to making $500,000 in 12 months—and how you can successfully apply the very same process to your business.

FROM A ME-TOO BRAND TO BADASS

We narrowed our target audience, our offerings, and our message. We focused on a market we knew and liked best: one- to three-person service businesses. We dusted off one of our small afterthought services and made it our company's focal point. We changed all our messaging and copy to reflect our newfound niche.

As soon as we made the switch, our lives changed in some critical ways:

- Old prospects that previously weren't going to close turned into excited clients.
- We whittled down prospect calls to 15 minutes. No more coffee meetings, follow-ups, proposals, or free strategy sessions. No more proposals = no more free work!
- Instead of free proposals, we got paid to pitch.
- No more annoying, random client emails and requests sucking up our time.
- No more design by committee!
- Suddenly we were getting prospects out of the blue. People heard about our process and

wanted it NOW. Once we were full of clients, we started raising prices.

- I stopped working on weekends and I stopped networking.
- We made $500,000 in 12 months without paying for advertising.

One reason we were able to attract so much work is that we implemented these tactics and philosophies for all of our clients too, and they got similar results. The methods apply to any solopreneur or small service business where the goal is to attract hungry, excited clients who are willing to pay a premium to hire you.

WHO THE HELL AM I?

I'll let you in on a little secret: *I hate the branding industry.* I think it's convoluted and difficult to understand. It's full of misinformation and generalizations that trick small business owners into going down the wrong path. People refer to "branding" as one idea that can be applied to any business, but it can't. This misinformation confuses small business owners and results in a lot of wasted time and money.

I didn't study branding, communications, or design. I've never worked for an agency or apprenticed with a brand strategist. In fact, I didn't even know what the hell branding was when we started our company.

And yet here I am about to school you on how to build your own Badass Brand. Why would you listen to me? Because of my real-world experience successfully crafting Badass Brands for myself and for hundreds of successful clients just like you. I haven't been tainted by the so-called "rules" of the branding industrial complex. These cookie-cutter applications of brand pyramids or spider diagrams might be necessary for large corporate brands, but they don't apply well to small businesses that need tactical steps to build a brand that attracts clients.

The problem with most alleged branding info is that it's generic and nonspecific. Statements like "Lead with the WHY," for example. What the hell does that mean, *in practice*, for your business? A lot of people go into business for themselves because they want to support themselves while helping others. But that goal in and of itself isn't going to turn acquaintances into clients.

We define Badass Brands as those that command a premium price and attract ideal clients. They are able to do this because they are noticeable, memorable, and shareable.

However, finding that for yourself can be difficult. So we've developed a process and a series of formulas that walk you through how to find the intersection of all the aspects that make you different. They are all derived from things that you *actually* think and do. This is *not* about making something up.

Instead, it's about identifying your expertise at something clear, specific, and unique to you. All aspects of the formulas require you to narrow down, pick the best pieces, toss the rest, and focus. Some show you how to turn what you already do into an actual product.

When you turn your expertise and ideas into something tangible that other people can understand, it can finally start making you money. (Yes, I *promise* you have a lot of potential opportunities right now, and I'm going to help you find them.)

WHY THE TIME IS *NOW* FOR A BADASS BRAND

We all know there is a lot of economic uncertainty and fear these days. Technology is advancing at exponential rates, threatening the stability that many of us were raised to covet. Understanding how to capitalize on your knowledge is the new way to get that stability back. Whereas stocks, real estate, or corporate jobs are precarious, nothing can take away your information and experience. And you can always increase the value of this incredible asset—*for free.*

Badass Branding is about reclaiming control over your financial destiny by giving you a simple way to make money with little to no overhead. Freedom is the new benchmark for wealth. And there is nothing more freeing than knowing your most valuable income-producing asset is *your* expertise.

Badass Branding creates the structure to turn expertise into profit. You can start selling immediately, with relatively little effort. I love service businesses because I'm impatient. I lose motivation if I can't see a quick path to profitability. These start-up companies that spend months or years developing their product and looking for funding scare me. That's just not my style—and if you're reading this book, I'm guessing it's not yours either.

The beauty of learning these skills is that once you do it successfully and understand the formula, you'll be able to replicate it for your other skills forever after.

Many of the things I teach in this book will likely scare you because they may ask you to step outside your comfort zone. They are easier said than done. But the act of being scared and doing it anyway is what will separate you from every other struggling entrepreneur. Only the bold can have a Badass Brand that attracts clients and commands a premium price.

I've had clients question these tactics. They've told me that their industry is different, so these methods cannot and do not apply to them. And sometimes they don't. But more often, the golden opportunity is the very fact that nobody else in your industry is doing this. When it's not common and you do it first, you are building a Badass Brand.

Do you want to putter along like most other self-employed people, always looking for your next client? Networking constantly to stay top of mind of your referral partners? Always trying to sell instead of having confidence that the right opportunities will close themselves...and you'll make more money because of it? Some people can't hack it, but if you saw this book and related to its sassy messaging, I know you can.

WHO THIS BOOK IS FOR

When you are always putting out fires—or when your to-do list is always a little too long—you never have the time to build the processes and value in your business that allow you to charge more. And you will always be stuck there unless you take the steps necessary to get out of that rut.

- If you love what you do and you want to share it with others...
- If you know how valuable you are, and how much your expertise can change other people's lives and businesses...
- If you still want to improve, because even

though you are good, you want to become even greater...

- If you want to get hired by fans who love and respect your opinion and advice...
- If you want clients to hire you for what you do best...
- If you want to get paid more than your competitors, and still win the business...

...then you need a *Badass Brand.*

"SUCCESS" AND THE STORIES IN THIS BOOK

Success means different things to different people, but one thing is certain: You'll never achieve success if you don't know what it means to you. For example, we could have listened to the many business coaches that suggested we hire teams, teach them our process, and scale up our model. But for us, success is freedom, and we don't want employees. So instead, we are constantly looking for ways to increase the value of our services without a staff. As we are able to increase our prices, we can decrease the number of projects we work on, which frees up more time which gives us more freedom in our lives. Finding the right balance is our goal.

Your definition of success might be *all about the benjamins,* and that's cool! Put a number on it (we'll go into this in more depth in Chapter 5). But outside of money, it's good to write a more comprehensive definition of success from the start so you know when you've achieved it. Defining success as "making as much money as I can" is quite limiting, and pretty vague. If you leave it open-ended, you will never really get there. And you'll spend your life constantly striving for more, missing your achievements along the way.

The success stories in this book are here to bring the ideas to life. Some are about our clients, and some merely illustrate the points. But in every case, the outcomes are directly related to what success means to the individual—and, just as important, to their effort and commitment. Execution is everything. You have to believe more in yourself and your abilities than in whatever Tom, Dick, or Harry has to say in the short term about you.

That's what Badasses do.

SHAKE YOUR BADASS

I learn by doing. I love business books, but I'm usually implementing the new ideas I've read about before I've even finished the chapter. Because that approach has worked for me, I encourage you to do the same.

At the end of each chapter, answer the short series of questions. Research proves that you're 10 times more likely to do something if you write it down, so let's take the first step together! Answer the following questions to get started:

- What is your favorite thing to do and sell?
- What is the most profitable thing you do and sell?
- Are they the same thing? Can you imagine building a business around just selling that?
- Who are your favorite past clients? Explain why they are your favorites. Imagine if all your clients were like these clients.

Download the supplemental workbook at **badassyourbrand.com/workbook**, a great place to document your thoughts and next steps, with a few added surprises!

CHAPTER ONE

LOVE + PROFIT = BADASSERY

Steve and I started Worstofall Design in our little railroad-style Brooklyn apartment in 2011. Steve was a graphic designer, and I was an aspiring entrepreneur with a knack for figuring things out, so we decided that I would run the business side of things and allow him to focus his time on doing what he did best: designing.

Our goal was to support ourselves completely while working from home. If we could make $100,000 in a year, we would consider ourselves wildly successful. In 2012, our first full year in business, we hit $100,000—woo-hoo!

We were rich, and feeling pretty good about ourselves. But we got taken down a peg after reading the classic business book *The E-Myth*, which informed me that I didn't, in fact, own a business. *I owned a job.*

Feeling deflated, I told Steve we needed to hire a team. After all, we had started this because we *didn't* want jobs.

And that's when we looked at all the successful agencies around us, companies we looked up to, and tried to model what they were doing. With no background in hiring or management, we hired a couple of enthusiastic young go-getters to build our team.

We continued to emulate what we saw our competition doing. We would see a proposal, a deck, or a portfolio, or just a new agency website, and stop everything we were doing because we felt like we needed that shiny new object to succeed. We once saw an agency website video that was so cool, we dropped our work and spent two days trying to shoot our own. Another time, we stopped in our tracks and spent two full days writing and designing a 30-page deck about our company after a colleague showed us theirs.

In retrospect, we were always copying other companies because we were struggling to find clients and we didn't know what else to do. So when we saw someone else doing something that impressed us, we immediately thought that must be the reason we weren't getting clients.

Steve and I had two years in business under our

belts, so we felt confident that our process and work were solid and we could justify raising our prices— which was a good thing, because we needed more money coming in. Our overhead had doubled with the employees. We also hired them before we could afford to do so, with almost no reserves in the bank. We had to get juicier contracts to pay the extra overhead, and thought the $30,000 to $50,000 price tags that our competitors were charging were also what we needed to create stability. And, as with almost every decision we had made together since we met, we just went for it.

But as the price increased, it got harder and harder to close. And then, *crickets*.

We didn't know that we had made a critical and all-too-common mistake: We looked at how other companies operated in the market, and we tried to copy them. Every time a competitor did something that impressed us, we tried to replicate it. We were a "me-too brand", and that just makes you a less impressive version of the company you're trying to copy.

That's how I ended up sitting on the kitchen floor in tears in March 2014, in debt and faced with the possibility of having to admit failure. We were acting on ideas without understanding *why* we were implementing them. We were allocating time to projects based on what agencies did, and it was costing us dearly.

So what turned it around? What enabled us to go from debt to highly profitable in less than a year?

Figuring out what made us unique and special.

And this is how we did it.

LESSON #1: LOVE + PROFIT = BADASSERY

There are two cornerstones to our philosophy: (1) you have to be totally in love with your small business to be successful, and (2) a business without profit is not a business; it's a job without security.

Building a business is hard work no matter what. Why would you put all that effort into doing something you don't even like that much? Why would you bust your butt finding projects that put you to sleep?

It sounds obvious, but after the initial thrill of going out on your own is gone and it's time to pay the bills, many people just default into a series of decisions that leave them with a lackluster business that stops inspiring them. Then they lack the enthusiasm they had when they started it.

We were committing both cardinal sins. When we were forced to reevaluate our company, we found out that neither of us really enjoyed what we were doing, and it was not profitable.

This meant it was time for us to look inside ourselves and determine what we love about what we do.

- What did we really, truly love about our business?
- Why did we get into business in the first place?
- Which exact aspects of our business got us hyped each day to jump out of bed and take on the world?

Thankfully, we realized we really *did* love the actual work. Steve is an artist at heart, and that makes him a Badass graphic designer. He can become so engrossed in projects that he will not move his butt off the chair or even look up for hours at a time.

And I love working with clients. I am energized by their goals, and I thrive on understanding their challenges and creating a complete plan to get them where they want to go. I've been likened to a business strategist as much as a branding strategist, and I admit I do a ton of business strategy with clients—because I also love small businesses!

When I see a company in need of branding help, there is usually a business challenge that needs solving as well. I love that I bring expertise from a variety of disciplines, so instead of just solving the problem they *think* they have, I can diagnose the problem they *actually* have—and bring a fully formed solution that will solve it, not just give them a pretty new website (which usually doesn't solve the main problem).

Great—so we knew we loved the meat of what we did. But we also had to look at what we *didn't* like about our industry.

Most branding exercises focus on answering the question "What do you stand for?" While this is a great question in theory, most people come up with pretty wimpy answers, like "I stand for *honesty.*" "I stand for *integrity.*" "I stand for *great customer service.*"

Sure, I stand for those things too! Do you know anybody who *doesn't* think, say, or want those things? Probably not, which makes this a not-very-useful question.

Instead, we asked ourselves: *What do you stand against?*

- What pisses you off most about your industry?
- What do you hate about your industry that you think you could do better?
- Which parts specifically drag you down and make you watch the clock?

When we asked ourselves these questions we realized we didn't like the very model we were actively trying to build in our business—the agency model! That is, we didn't like managing ongoing clients because that meant we had to adhere to business hours. Ongoing clients meant we could never really check out while on vacation.

We also didn't want employees anymore. But delegating client management to employees is how most business owners are able to go on vacation and disconnect from their business from time to time, so this caused a bit of a dilemma.

We also didn't like how much red tape and project management were required for the large clients we were going after. They often felt like a huge waste of time and resources. We had a hunch that if the clients didn't need so much management, meetings, and rounds of feedback, projects could cost a fraction of the price and time—and headache.

We loved the first part—the big, imaginative brainstorming and work creation. But we hated the months of revisions and the committees of opinions that watered down the work. Steve would pour his soul into projects, and clients would love them—yet still change everything until they were unrecognizable. And all the while, I was managing and placating them with calls and meetings.

This didn't sit well with Steve's drive to create, or my impatience to move the needle forward. We wanted more of the good stuff, and less of the stuff that weighed us down.

Finally, we had to take a cold hard look at the books and talk money. We asked ourselves:

- What is the most profitable thing we sell?
- Are any of our projects even profitable?

We were charging $30,000 to $50,000 for a full branding project, which sounds like a lot of money for a small business. But we had to support salaries for ourselves and two employees. And because we were optimistic about our abilities—and saw ourselves as awesome bosses who didn't take young twenty-somethings for granted by paying them unlivable wages (yes, a little naïve)—we were paying them a lot.

That high overhead plus the endless hours these projects took over the course of four, six, sometimes 12 months meant that there was no money left over at the end of the year. And that is the definition of unprofitable.

But we did have this offering that we had created and then paid little attention to for more than a year.

As we had started to raise our prices, we realized that the network of small business owner clients we'd amassed over the years could no longer afford our services. We had priced ourselves out of a large group of people who had become fans of our work.

So in 2013, on a challenge from our business coach, Evan Horowitz, we tried to come up with a product specifically for these fans. What would we be willing to deliver for, say, a $3,000 budget?

That's when we developed something we called "the Brandup."

We realized we had been overcomplicating the

project because we thought the agency model required it. We figured that if someone hired us for a $40,000 project, we had to prove we had done 60 hours of exploration, created hundreds of logo variations, and presented our top three. After all, they were paying us to do that kind of exploration and research—right?

But just because that's how agencies work doesn't mean it's the most effective approach. More often than not, the designs Steve made in the first few hours would make it to the final presentation—even after exploring hundreds of logos and variations.

Our clients didn't know they were inflating their own price tag with those expectations, and neither did we. But if they could commit ahead of time to trusting us and our opinions, they could get the same level of work for a lot less money. And if they trusted us to do good work, we wouldn't have to do 60 hours of due diligence. And we thought maybe some people with smaller budgets would be willing to trust us.

So the Brandup was born. It was a one-day project where clients would just buy our time—$2,995 for the day—and we would make them as much work as we could. Clients understood that the faster they made decisions, the more design work they would get.

We all benefited from a shared impatience.

Those early clients got a logo, a one- to two-page

website, business cards, and a lesson on Squarespace. This gave them the tools to build the rest of the site themselves and control it in the future.

But they also got our expertise. We interviewed them, then showed them which design would actually achieve their goals. They weren't paying for graphic designers; they were paying for *branders* to show them the way.

This product was slow to start. We didn't even advertise it on our website. At the time, our forward-facing message focused on the fact that we did bigger projects. We didn't want to water that down with a small-business $3,000 product offering.

So we made a separate, unlinked page that I used as a secret weapon. I would tell potential clients we charged at least $30,000 for projects, and see how they reacted. If this was out of their price range, I would tell them about the Brandup.

BRANDUPS WERE OUR MOST PROFITABLE OFFERING!

Back to that night at the kitchen table, when we realized our intensive Brandups were much more profitable than the higher-paying projects. We were making a lot more money at $3,000 per day than when we had a $30,000 project over six months.

This isn't intuitive to many solopreneurs, so let me break it down another way. If a six-month project required us to work 10 full days, then both projects would be equally profitable. In that scenario, we would be getting paid $3,000 for one day of work.

But these six-month projects required way, way, *way* more than 10 days of work. And the work was hard to quantify. In addition to the creative work, project management became intensive for six-month projects. In total, it was more like 20 to 30 full days of work.

But 30 days of Brandups would garner $90,000, not $30,000. See how much more profitable that is? Same amount of time, three times the money.

PROFITABLE, CHECK. But *did* we *like it?*

The good news is, we did. We enjoyed these projects more because they played to our strengths. Clients hired us for our expertise, not to be their graphic design hands. This meant they loved the work and signed off with little feedback—and were usually ecstatic to do so right then and there. The expectation was clearly set, so they were always delighted.

We loved that we no longer worked with committees. Groups tend to water down creative work to please the lowest common denominator. This process, on the other hand, allowed our work to shine.

We also loved that Brandups didn't require us to maintain ongoing clients. Instead, they gave us more freedom with our time, and allowed us to come and go as we pleased. This had been our goal all along, which we had forgotten somewhere along the way.

We took our own medicine when we decided to go for it. We would ONLY sell Brandups from now on.

BRANDUPS WERE OUR BADASS OPPORTUNITY

I've used this method time and again for success. When you have a small business, identifying your favorite part about it will help you craft a business that you love. In turn, this will ensure that your business is cared for, nurtured, and pumped full of unlimited enthusiasm from an owner who sees it as his or her greatest project.

Whenever your favorite thing to do is also your most profitable, you have a huge opportunity. When you focus on selling only the thing you love to do—the thing that also makes the most money—your entire business will become more profitable.

It's just basic math. If your time is filled with high- and low-profit work, your profitability will lie somewhere in the middle. If your time is filled with only high-profit work, your profitability will always be high.

I can hear you now: *But what if I can't get enough*

clients for my high-profit offering to fill my time?

This is why most entrepreneurs won't make this leap. They are scared.

But if you trust that there are enough clients out there to fill in the gaps, you will have the stamina to find them. Instead of selling *all* your services and wasting time getting paid for low-profit work, you first must understand that you can turn down that work and use the time to *find* the high-profit clients. And if you do this consistently, you will eventually fill your docket with only high-profit clients—and make your entire business more profitable.

It really is as simple as it sounds; there's just a gap between the commitment and the full docket of clients. And that gap is the reason most entrepreneurs won't do it.

Okay—but what if your favorite thing is *not* your most profitable thing?

They won't always be the same. But that's all right! Now that you know your favorite thing and understand profitability, there are ways you can increase that favorite thing's profitability—three in particular:

1. Increase the value of what you're selling.
2. Increase the price of what you're selling.
3. Decrease the time spent on what you're selling.

Generally, you will be doing a combination of these three steps.

For example, we started by offering Brandups for about $3,000 per day. As we did more of them, we learned ways to both improve the service and increase the value of what we were delivering. At first, we worked only that day without doing prep work ahead of time. But we realized that prep work helped us deliver a lot more value in the Brandup. Instead of a one- or two-page website, we could build *an entire website* in one day.

In order to do that, we had to have a much clearer picture of what the project would entail—which meant we needed to speak with the clients ahead of time. And that conversation evolved into its own product: the Brandshrink. All of our clients first do a Brandshrink, where we develop the big-picture strategy. Because we do that ahead of time, once the client signs off, we can get very far with the website before the Brandup even begins.

The price steadily increased from $3,000 for one day to $10,000 for a one day. It made sense, given that our clients were getting substantially more work from us: the high-level strategy and plan; the design and build of the entire brand; and the logo, website, identity materials, social media profiles, and all the messaging and copy on the site. We also provide consulting on how to market their brands moving forward.

I couldn't charge $10,000 for the initial package we were selling, but once I increased the value of the package, I could!

The other way to increase the profitability of your favorite thing is to decrease the time spent. We definitely increased the time we spend on a Brandup to increase the value. However, we also constantly reevaluate our process to decrease the time needed. Our goal is to spend time on high-value work, not menial tasks.

For example, we deliver our files in a package of folders that takes some time to set up. Each folder (logo, website, business cards, stationery) has three folders within for the raw files, the preview files, and the print-ready files. Some have more. We took the time to set up a skeleton Brandup folder we can use for every project. It has the InDesign template files for two different-size business cards, as well as the template for a rack card if that is part of the client's package.

Setting up the files is a low-value task we repeat each time, and that time adds up. If we had to go to the website and find the dimensions every time we design a rack card, we'd be wasting time.

Similarly, much of the pre-Brandup correspondence I have with clients is the same. So I wrote templates that I can adjust as necessary. Why rewrite the same email over and over? I'd rather spend that time coming up with amazing messaging and copy.

The beauty of specializing on a process for a focused market is that you can create these processes. The more you do the same kind of project, the more proficient you become. And while doing the same thing over and over may sound boring, I find it's quite the opposite. You can always improve your skills and what you do. Every project is an opportunity to make it even better and more valuable. Every client's particular challenges are slightly different, and we are always looking for ways to solve them in the most effective way. The tools in our toolbox increase with every project—and there's nothing boring about that.

CASE STUDY: ROSEMARY, HOLISTIC PT

Rosemary is an experienced and capable physical therapist. Like most PTs, she sells hourly sessions to work with patients. However, Rosemary isn't just a licensed physical therapist. She is also an acupuncturist and a nutritionist, and she is educated in mindfulness and meditation. Because she is certified and experienced in many related fields, she is able to use a holistic approach with her clients.

This holistic approach to healing is what makes

her different. And while Rosemary might be great at what she does, lots of physical therapists have learned multiple healing disciplines. As a potential client, it's hard to understand what sets her apart.

Rosemary loves working with patients, but she wants to make more money and she doesn't know how to except by working longer hours. She feels stuck, and she is frustrated.

When we asked her to identify her favorite thing to sell, she told us that she had recently flown to India to treat a bedridden client who had injured herself and could barely walk. She did intensive work with this client every day and addressed all aspects of her life and health. After just two weeks, Rosemary had completely healed her. The client was back to her previously active self.

Rosemary loved this case because it allowed her to fully use all her knowledge and gifts. And unlike the patients she sees weekly, this client healed right before her eyes. Weekly patients don't always follow her advice strictly or exactly, so they don't get the benefit of an in-depth treatment.

She was excited to see how powerful her work could be! After all, those experiences—where she can see the results of her work—are what got her into the healing space to begin with.

Rosemary also cited these intensive sessions as the most profitable thing she sells. Her entire trip to India was completely covered, and she was paid much more than she would ever make in two weeks at her practice.

Rosemary had a Badass Branding opportunity right in front of her. Instead of following the usual PT business model, she could brand and market these intensive healing sessions—and charge a hefty price. That high price was justified by the amount of time she would spend with a given patient, and the high value she would provide.

Instead of weekly clients, she would take on just a couple of intensive clients at a time, and charge whatever she wanted for their sessions. Instead of pitching her holistic approach to physical therapy, she could pitch intensive sessions that healed in *weeks* instead of months. Her target market was executives, athletes, and wealthy individuals whose time is quantifiably very valuable. Someone for whom a $40,000 fee to be back to work in four weeks instead of six months is a no-brainer.

By making this change, Rosemary's brand messaging became a lot more noticeable, memorable, and shareable. Her clients mostly come from referring doctors, but these doctors know a lot of PTs. This doctor-PT relationship must be built over time, but most doctors still have multiple options of great PTs to whom they can refer their patients.

But Rosemary's new method and approach allows her to stand out among these choices. She can reeducate the doctors in her network and explain that she now only works in this intensive manner, and that her ideal market includes the high-end clients who would be itching to pay whatever it takes to heal quickly.

This also gives her a unique and noticeable reason to reach out to doctors she doesn't yet know, as she has something special to share. She isn't just another PT looking to build a relationship generally for her own benefit; instead, she has a valuable resource to offer. New doctors will be grateful to know about her, because when the right client comes along, they will look like heroes for making the referral to Rosemary.

It's not that other PTs couldn't do this; they could. In fact, I'm sure if a patient *offered* any PT $40,000 to do intensive work for a month, most would jump at the chance.

But who would do that?

This is the power of suggestive selling. A person might want to heal quickly, but not know that this personalized service is an option. Nor would they know how much it should cost—or trust that a PT they hired to work in this manner would be able to show results.

However, it's a much different experience when Rosemary has a set fee, can explain how the process works and what results the client can expect, and has evidence from former clients. The client hires Rosemary because they trust her process and see her as an expert.

They aren't hiring an hourly PT to work with them more frequently; they are hiring someone who specializes in *healing people faster*.

In fact, sometimes just simply stating the benefit you offer is the best tagline: "Heal Faster" with Rosemary's Intensive Healing Methodology that "gets you from bedridden to running again in weeks instead of months."

SHAKE YOUR BADASS

Now that I've shared a little context, let's revisit the questions from the Introduction in more detail:

- What is your favorite thing to do and sell?
  - What part of your business gets you jumping out of bed?
- Who are your favorite past clients?
  - Why are they your favorite? Imagine if all your clients were like these clients.
- What do you stand against in your industry?
  - What do you hate about your industry that you think you could do better?
  - What do you hate about how you currently work?
- What is the most profitable thing you do and sell? (Remember, not necessarily your highest-priced offering!)
- What is your least profitable offering?

Don't forget to download the supplemental workbook at **badassyourbrand.com/workbook** so you can keep all your work in one Badass place!!

Now just take a minute and explore what you've been selling. Is there something you love to do that is *more* profitable—and could you *do only that*? Are some of your least favorite things also your least profitable offerings? Can you imagine a world where you didn't have to do the things that make you the least amount of money? How can you increase the profitability of your favorite thing by (1) increasing the value, (2) increasing the price, and (3) decreasing the time you spend on it?

WHAT DATING TAUGHT ME ABOUT BADASS BRANDING

It was a Sunday afternoon in October 2008. A group of us headed to The Blind Tiger on Bleecker Street in the West Village to meet up with our friend and her classmates from Miami Ad School.

"Love at first sight" is a bit of an overdramatization. However, it's no exaggeration that when I walked in and locked eyes with Steve, I promptly turned to my girlfriends and said, "Hands off, he's mine."

I've always been pretty good at identifying what I want.

Steve and I were immediately engrossed in conversation. At one point my friend pulled me aside and said, "Just so you know, he'll never date you"—alluding to a salacious past she had observed in Miami.

I laughed. I had just met this guy and he was totally adorable—let the cards fall where they may!

You see, in dating, I was always very upfront about who I am and what I wanted—and that often worked to my detriment. I was always looking for love and not shy about announcing it. This can be extremely scary for a lot of people. My girlfriends often chastised me for not playing the game better—for being too forward and not playing hard-to-get with those I liked most. I would learn later that this is a profound lesson that applies just as well to business.

My friend was not just warning me about Steve; she was also advising that I was likely to scare him away. She was saying, "Don't be who you usually are with this guy; he won't respond well, and you'll get hurt."

But we became inseparable as the night unfolded, ignoring our 10 friends as we sat at the end of a long table and talked. And over the next few weeks, we quickly fell in love. Later, he told me he was so smitten *because* I was open and honest, instead of playing games. The very thing that many women say scare guys away was the reason this beautiful and previously relationship-phobic man fell for me head over heels and never looked back.

In other words, in relationships I had a Badass Brand that repelled many but attracted my perfect, ideal match. And if we equate profit with love and happiness, I'm the richest woman on earth.

HOW YOU SHOW UP IN LIFE IS HOW YOU SHOW UP IN BUSINESS

My philosophy on dating has always been to focus on crafting your best, happiest self in order to find the perfect mate. I didn't hesitate to show who I was, because I was perfectly happy with who I was. But until you really know yourself, and are content with who you are and how you exist in the world, how will you ever meet someone who will love that best version of yourself?

You can't, and you won't.

I later realized that if I applied these same principles to business, I would garner similar results.

If you play games when you are dating someone, you will attract a partner who likes a crafted version of you. But an ideal mate loves you just the way you are. The one who matches up perfectly with your preferences. The one you love because he or she makes you better.

And this works perfectly in business as well. A lot of companies bend to their potential clients' will. A client wants their life coach to start advising on nutrition, so the coach pops open a couple of nutrition books and tries to deliver. A company wants you to present your work to the management team and let *them* present it to the owners, and you oblige even though you know it's not as effective as you presenting your work to the owners directly. A client wants it to be cheaper, and you bargain.

But nobody benefits from this wishy-washy approach. The client is left managing their own expectations, and when expectations aren't clearly laid out, they're usually higher than what a company plans to deliver.

The client is confused about why they aren't getting what they want, and they begin to nag. The woman is upset because the man isn't calling her enough, but she doesn't want to be the kind of girl who needs too much attention. The guy is upset because the girl is being passive-aggressive and he doesn't know what he did wrong.

What my friends who played the game didn't understand was that I was acting the way I was on purpose. An aloof woman I am not. When I want something, I go after it. And I wanted and needed a man who not only wasn't scared by that, but also liked it. It's who I am, so why would I try to attract someone who disliked that part of me? That would require me to hide who I am, until, of course, my real self eventually emerged.

My approach to dating scared away quite a few guys. I won't lie; it hurt. I was ghosted here and there by men who undoubtedly thought I was coming on too strong.

But you need to find only that one person who completes you in life—so really, who cares? Ten months after I broke up with my previous boyfriend, I met the man I would marry and start a business with. The night we met, my friend had warned me—with the best intentions—that he wasn't the dating type. And as

I would learn, he wasn't—until he met me.

In love, you need only one ideal client to make a fortune. A Badass Brand might need a few more, but if they love and respect what you do—and will pay you handsomely for it—you don't need that many. And you can afford to repel the rest.

Indeed, that's part of what makes your brand so very Badass.

"Well, you were right, it's clogged.
What should we do?"

CHAPTER TWO

THE BADASS SECRET TO CHARGING MORE

When Steve and I started building a graphic design agency, we truly believed our work was good. He was a lifelong artist, and had studied plein air Impressionist painting with a few masters before double majoring in art and art history in college.

It's worth noting that when I hear "double-major," I usually think "overachiever," but Steve in no way considers himself an overachiever. He originally majored in fine art, with a focus on painting. Yet he had taken so many of the art history classes by senior year that he had already completed all the requirements to double major—so he did. That pretty much sums up Steve's work ethic: he considers himself a head-in-the-cloud creative, yet he can get so laser focused and lost in his work that he accidentally double majors in college and graduates with a high GPA—despite having the stoner reputation that got him the nickname "Worstofall."

After college, Steve tried to live off his art—both in Boston with CU friends, and then in Amsterdam on his cousin Alies' couch. When neither scenario worked out, his family urged him to consider pursuing a slightly more lucrative path in graphic design, so he enrolled in Miami Ad School for two years and applied his art skills to the computer.

Because of this breadth of education in art and design, and my background in startups and entrepreneurial ventures, we felt that our work was at least on par with—if not better than—most of what was out there.

When it came time for me to sell our services, I touted Steve's art background as the thing that made us different. It wasn't a great pitch, because it relied heavily on people loving our work, and a lot of great graphic designers have beautiful work.

Clients had a lot of options, and who do people usually decide to hire when they have many choices that feel similar?

They decide based on price.

It's a race to the bottom when you are a service

provider that looks like everyone else. When everything else is equal, why *wouldn't* a buyer go with the lowest-priced company?

When you haven't made a case for being better than the competition, that's exactly the situation you will be in: compared to a bunch of competitors who are all selling the same thing, with price as the defining factor. And when the decision comes down to price, two things can happen:

1. You lose the business to someone cheaper.
2. You win the business because *you* are the cheapest, and quickly become overworked and underpaid.

This is what happens when potential clients view you as a service provider, and it is probably the reason most solopreneurs struggle to close clients, find themselves bargaining on price to close the deal, or lose clients to cheaper competitors.

I know how frustrating that is because we dealt with it for years, and—as I mentioned—we became overworked and got into debt.

LESSON #2: INSTEAD, POSITION YOURSELF AS AN EXPERT

You may or may not be great at what you do, but

the sale is more about how you present yourself. Sometimes people hocking crap are highly skilled at marketing, and they can beat out those of us who truly take pride in our work. But that's how the world works—and if you ignore this part of the game, *you will lose.*

If you create value in the world, it's your job to market yourself well enough to ensure your people have access to the valuable services they need. If you fail at communicating your value, your *clients* will lose when they end up hiring a less valuable competitor because they didn't understand why *you* are better.

How you describe your services, what you charge, and how you charge communicate a lot about your level of skill. I meet so many people who want to be experts, thought leaders, or gurus—yet their pricing and sales process tell a different story.

HOW TO CHARGE LIKE A BADASS EXPERT

Here is the difference between an expert and a service provider: Experts learn their trade over a lifetime, and service providers execute ideas primarily based on direction from the client.

Most people who charge based on time are service providers. Even if they are proposing a project rate, they formulate that rate based on a forecasted amount of time needed.

In contrast, an expert's fee is related to the value of their contribution. They know how long it will take because they've done it a million times, but they don't charge based on that time. They have spent years, sometimes a lifetime, learning a trade—and clients pay for that knowledge regardless of how long it takes.

Imagine a plumber. I've had a plumber snake my clogged drain in 10 minutes and charge $200. And while the price tag shocked me at first, I soon realized it was completely worth it. He knows how to solve my problem, and I don't. He knew exactly what to do, didn't ask me how, and came when I needed him. That's *value*.

BUILDING YOUR PROCESS LIKE A BADASS

Service providers are the *hands*: They execute. They ask, "What do you want? What do you think? Do you like this?"

Experts are the *brain*: They tell you why a decision is right and offer thoughtful reasoning and innovative ideas to back it up. They say, "Here's how to achieve your goals based on your current situation and challenges."

Service providers have to put guidelines and restrictions on their work to regulate the potential for a deluge of client-change requests.

Experts establish similar guidelines, but typically

don't need to enforce them. Clients are in the expert's hands, and are looking to the expert to lead the way.

Web designers, for example, are often service providers. They ask for pages needed, content, photos, and other websites as examples; they are acting as the hands for your vision.

But when web designers are experts, they ask what the client is looking to accomplish. They discuss the brand, the market, the current site content. They ask about the goals so they can use their expertise in web design to achieve those goals.

When experts ask these questions, they can charge a premium. After all, it costs more to tell the client how a website should look and function than to simply put things in place based on client notes. For example, expert web designers will tell the client what pieces of content they need in advance, and recommend additional outside help if necessary.

PROVIDING RESULTS LIKE A BADASS

Both experts and service providers strive for you to be happy; however, experts are less likely to sacrifice the truth to make you feel good. As in, that dress really *does* make you look fat.

High-level consultants are a great example. When corporations hire Diane DiResta to train their C-Suite

Executives in communication skills that will make them prominent leaders in their companies, she takes the lead. And sometimes she has to tell these people— executives who are probably used to hearing yes from people they hire—things they *don't* want to hear. But Diane would be doing them a disservice if she just made them feel good. They hire her to tell the truth, and although it sometimes may be hard to hear, she knows they will ultimately achieve their goals if they listen.

If you're positioning yourself as an expert, you're in the driver's seat. You are able to deliver your top value because it sets up the framework for clients to listen. And when you are able to deliver top value to clients, you can charge top dollar.

When we moved away from quoting projects based on hourly work and started only working in a set process with a flat fee, *we immediately shifted our positioning from service provider to expert.* Instead of just claiming we were better because Steve has artistic sensibilities, we could demonstrate that expertise through our tried-and-true process and relatively high prices. Although most people contact us with a list of deliverables they think they need, we start with questions about their ultimate goals. When we understand the bigger picture, we are better able to guide them to achieve their desired results—which sometimes involves telling them things they don't want to hear. But being an expert voice of reason—someone who is not there to just say yes to a paying client, but who has enough understanding of the problem to make sure the goals are achieved—creates trust. Because we communicate this clearly upfront, clients hire us for our expertise, not just our design skills. And that creates a successful dynamic for all.

CASE STUDY: PRIYA AND ROB, FINANCIAL ADVISORS

I met Priya and Rob about a year into their budding business. Two financial planners from Merrill Lynch, this husband-and-wife duo left corporate America to chase the dream. They wanted to be their own bosses and live the good life. A mutual friend and colleague introduced us because, as he said, he could tell they needed what we were selling.

The first thing Priya told me was that she loved that we were also a husband-and-wife team. They could see themselves in the copy on our website. They too were trying to change their industry, and felt like the rebel Davids in a world of Goliaths. But unlike us, they had identified the industry problem they were trying to solve before they even started their company.

They were frustrated that Merrill helped only the extremely wealthy with financial planning. They saw a great need for financial services among their friends: young professionals with budding successful careers but no financial know-how.

They found themselves constantly relaying the financial advice they gave to their clients to their friends—for free. There was a clear business opportunity.

They left their jobs to start their own business, then called Moderna Capital. They hired a design company and put up a nice shiny website. They told everyone they knew that they had opened their doors to young professionals in need of financial advice. They were excited to build a business to help.

For a year, they did what they had learned—and what had worked—at Merrill: They wined and dined and schmoozed with friends and acquaintances to build trust. They networked and socialized, trying to gauge the perfect time to bring up their services and explain how they could help.

But they just couldn't get clients. Tactics that had worked for acquiring millionaires and billionaires at Merrill Lynch were not working on these twenty- and thirtysomethings. Not even friends and family—who already knew, liked, and trusted them—would sign on!

Priya and Rob came to us disillusioned and confused. They had spent a lot of their savings to get this business off the ground, yet had never signed a paying client. Plus, they just didn't like what they were doing. Every meeting was uncomfortable. They could feel people recoil when they mentioned that they were financial planners. And when they *did* get interest from a potential client, follow-ups could go on for months— but when it came time to discuss payment, they never heard back.

These two are everything you could ask for in Badass Business owners. Highly intelligent and expert in their field, they were both VPs at Merrill by the time they were in their mid-twenties. They *know* what they're doing. But they're not the stuffy corporate type. They can discuss fashion, hot new restaurants, or the best hotels in Paris, then quickly switch to conversation about Buddhism, cooking, or relationships. Eloquent and polished in their presentation and appearance, they are fun and friendly while still professional.

So why wouldn't anyone hire them? Because from the outside, they looked like just another wealth manager—and NYC is *teeming* with them. It was too easy to compare them to the thousands of others.

We weren't surprised when they told us they charged a little less than the big competitors. In fact, they used this as a selling tactic. They told potential clients that because they didn't have the huge overhead, they could pass that savings.

They were lowering their price to try to compete with other wealth managers when all other things were equal. But unfortunately, even that wasn't working—because all other things *weren't* equal. They were small and seemingly untested (even though they had proven themselves at Merrill Lynch), and when it comes to managing money, most people are reluctant to hire a small, unestablished firm.

They were providing a service, and they weren't measuring up on the comparison chart.

TURNING MODERNA CAPITAL INTO STASH WEALTH, AND STASH WEALTH INTO EXPERTS

First, we had to help Priya and Rob get real about what they were and weren't selling.

They thought they were selling financial advice. Showing young professionals that it's never too early to start a retirement account. Explaining why compound interest is your best friend.

Right—because *that's what my friends and I are talking about at dinner parties.* Nope.

In this way, their services were interchangeable with other wealth managers, and positioned them as service providers. However, who they were and what they were trying to change about the industry were expert-level services.

Remember, they started the company because they were fed up with Merrill Lynch, which works only with people who have a minimum of $500,000 in liquid assets. They knew that people of their generation with thriving careers *also* need access to reliable financial advisors and advice. Indeed, they are less likely to build that kind of wealth without sound advice.

Unlike the Goliaths of the industry, Priya and Rob *were* their market. They understood what makes people of their generation tick, what they are interested in, how they speak, what keeps them up at night. As wealth managers, they were one of many. But as voices of their generation in the wealth-management world, they were *experts*.

But they hadn't presented themselves that way. They were a me-too brand, following the Merrill Lynch blueprint they had learned. They were selling the same services in the same way, but to a different crowd. They were schooled in corporate America, so they were scared to color outside the lines. Their name, Moderna Capital, was a perfect indicator of the belief that they needed to fit in to the industry.

They were against many of the things big corporate Merrill Lynch stood for, yet they had built a brand that looked and sounded *a lot* like Merrill. The copy was a little more hip, but it didn't reflect the passion they expressed when they spoke about their disagreement with how Merrill Lynch does business.

And that was exactly where their opportunity lay.

You see, Priya is a whip-smart, sassy woman. She's in the know when it comes to the hottest restaurant in Manhattan, the latest fashion trend, the hippest clubs. She lives the life her clients aspire to, but she wasn't speaking their language.

We encouraged them to embrace their authenticity. Don't say it like Merrill Lynch is censoring you; say it in your voice. Talk about happy hour and pop culture. Speak to your clients like you're one of them, not a slightly younger version of corporate America. If they wanted that, they would hire Merrill Lynch.

You can't compete with Merrill, so don't even try. Offer the market something different, so there is a distinct choice between them and you.

And that difference comes from within.

Well, this sounded exciting *in theory,* but when we told Priya and Rob they should rename their company and call their newsletter "Financial Cliffnotes: Get Your Financial Sh*t Together," they almost had a heart attack.

"We can't say that. People won't take us seriously."

"You don't understand our industry, Pia; people won't trust us if we talk like that."

Oh, *really?*

When we asked about their process for onboarding clients, they explained that first you built relationships in the financial world. You gain trust, and finally onboard a client's money once they agree to sign on with you. Only at this point would they assess the client's financial situation in detail, build a plan, and then put it into action.

This might work for older people who have lots of wealth, but they were trying to sign younger clients. The generation they were trying to attract has a different relationship with both money and purchasing. The idea of marrying a financial planner before you even have a test drive sounds scary. Plus, this market has probably never done anything with their cash before. Choosing their financial advisor is a big decision—and they likely don't have any experience in assessing who they should work with.

There are too many unknowns, and that causes paralysis when trying to make a decision.

We suggested that they flip the process on its head. Instead of trying to convince clients to sign over all their assets, why not sell the financial plans as a product *first*? They were in the market to address millennials' lack of access to sound financial advice. They could solve this problem for a flat fee, and in a way that would be more attractive to their market—more in line with how they purchase.

At first this didn't make any sense to Priya. Financial plans are usually *included* in the management fee, and they were targeting clients with *less* money, so why would they expect clients to now pay for it upfront?

We were asking them to take a completely different approach: meeting the clients where they currently are. Instead of trying to convince millennials about the importance of a Roth IRA, they could get their clients' finances in order, help them understand their financial situation, and explain what they needed to do financially in order to achieve what they wanted in life.

Now that sounds pretty attractive, especially for a flat fee. Clients could get the solution without tying themselves to a company for life.

They somewhat reluctantly agreed, and we designed them a Stash Plan™. For a flat fee, a client could hire them to "get their financial sh*t together."

To be honest, it was slow to start. It didn't seem like Priya believed it would work, so she wasn't really selling it.

But then it started to snowball. The Stash Plan™ was specific, different, easy to remember, and therefore easy to talk about with others. As time went on, they got more and more referrals. And then Priya wrote a guest article for Refinery 29 on the first of the year that just hit. Suddenly they were getting dozens of inquiries a day. They were immediately operating at maximum capacity; at the time, they could service only eight Stash Plans™ per month.

They quickly hired their first employee and raised the price. The well didn't dry up. Ever since, they've been consistently making well over $20,000 per month just on Stash Plans™. Remember, initially *they weren't going to even charge for this service.* And they didn't build it just to make money; they did it to change the sales process and position themselves as experts.

Fast forward a few years later: Priya is a regular guest on SiriusXM. She was invited to speak at Cornell and Harvard Business School. She is the financial voice for Bustle and the chief financial expert for Refinery 29, and is represented on a slew of other high-traffic blogs for millennials. Large financial-services firms regularly contact her trying to get information they are paying huge consulting firms to tell them: *How the hell do we reach millennials?*

They are the only company in the world that offers a Stash Plan™. Maybe other companies offer something similar (I'm sure they will once this book comes out), but nobody offers a Stash Plan™.

Another thing the Stash Plan™ accomplished was to get Priya to stop wining and dining clients to get their business. Now, after building and presenting the Stash Plan™ to potential clients, she gives them two options: (1) implement the plan themselves or (2) sign on the dotted line and let Stash take over.

More than 90 percent of Stash Plan™ clients don't even blink. After the amazing experience of working with Stash, they naturally want to move forward.

The original goal was to sign clients for wealth management. Instead, they sell Stash Plans™ and get paid to pitch their services, make $20,000 (or more) per month doing it, and onboard about 18 clients per month. (These numbers are based on Stash Wealth's situation as of the writing of this book. I have no doubt that by the time you read this, these numbers have at least doubled based on their current growth trajectory.)

Priya and Rob positioned themselves as experts in their market by providing a solution service that nobody else does, which solves a specific problem in their market. They owned their brand voice and didn't care that the industry might not get it.

And this transformed them from service providers to experts.

They had to get comfortable with the uncomfortable. They had to ignore the friends and family who were telling them that their offering was inappropriate for the industry, that they were doing it wrong, that they needed to watch XYZ company and copy it.

But here's what we know: If it weren't uncomfortable, it wouldn't be different. In fact, if it's not uncomfortable, you can be pretty sure you are still just another me-too brand in your industry.

And that *wouldn't* be badass.

SHAKE YOUR BADASS

Be honest with yourself: Are you positioning yourself as a service provider or an expert?

- What's your process for working with clients?
- What do you normally do for free and how can you charge for it?
- What about it is the same each time?
- What parts can you streamline?
- What's your unique point of view?
- Forget what's appropriate, forget what others are doing, and go with your gut. What are you bringing to the table that other people aren't?
- How do you charge?
- How can you turn your hourly services into a flat-rate product? (I'll go into detail on this soon.)

Haven't download the supplemental workbook yet? What are you waiting for?!
badassyourbrand.com/workbook
Because Badasses take ACTION.

WHAT OUR FIRST DATE TAUGHT ME ABOUT BADASS BRANDING

I met Steve the week he moved to NYC. As I mentioned in the previous chapter, we were quickly drawn to each other and scheduled a first date for the following week.

Steve had just moved here; I was born and raised in the East Village. Did I ask him what he wanted to do on our date? Of course not! As an *expert* New Yorker, I knew it was my job to put together an impressive itinerary of insider hot spots.

Neither of us had any money, so I had to plan an intriguing date that didn't cost an arm and a leg. I knew he was an artist, so with a "dignified quarter" (as my art teacher at Hunter High School called it), I took him to the bar on the roof of the Metropolitan Museum of Art to sip a beer next to some oversized Jeff Koons animal balloons. I followed up that impressive and classy spot with a few locals-only joints in the Village, including a sushi bar on St. Marks that is both delicious and crazy affordable.

Now imagine if I asked him what he wanted to do. His uninformed requests may have landed us at an overpriced hotel bar in midtown Manhattan full of out-of-towners showing off or, worse, a TGI Fridays.

Therein lies the difference between an expert and a

service provider.

Like any expert, had I been charging for my expertise I certainly would have gotten top dollar. Secret little spots are not easily found in Zagat and Frommers; they are known only from a lifetime of living in the city.

"Seriously?"

CHAPTER THREE

SELLING IS NOT BADASS

When we started Worstofall Design, the first place I went looking for clients was Craiglist. I had found odd jobs there before and it was the only place I knew to look.

I searched for graphic design gigs, logo design postings, and the like. And at first, I didn't get many replies. One day I decided to post a job exactly like the ones I thought we were perfect for, just to take a look at the competition: "Logo design needed for small business."

Within minutes, my email box was flooded. Within an hour I had received more than 100 submissions. Most of them looked and sounded exactly the same, like a copied-and-pasted email that was being sent to any and every posting remotely related to graphic design.

Many went like this:

Subject: *re: Logo design needed for small business*

Email text: *To Whom It May Concern,*

My name is <u>NAME</u> *and I am a professional graphic designer. I saw on Craigslist that you are looking for a logo designer for your business. I am excellent fit for your job and I am an expert in designing the logos. You can see my Portfolio on the link below: website.com*

Well, now it all made sense. I was *also* sending these very dry emails, and they were getting completely lost in the fray. And you don't care anymore after you read three of these; you just want to see the work. So I changed my emails to this:

Subject: *The Worst Logo Designer*

Email text: *worstofalldesign.com*

That was it. Now that I knew what I was competing with, I knew my email had to stand out. They didn't care that I was interested in the work (would I be reaching out if I wasn't?) or that I came across their listing (clearly); they just wanted to see the work.

I started getting many more responses. The subject

line caught my potential clients' attention in an inbox full of the generic ones, and it sparked just enough curiosity to click the link. After that, because the work was good, we got inquiries.

NOT SELLING

We were selling ourselves hard when we first started, like many other Craigslisters. We were desperate for the gig—and when you really want to sell someone your services, you tend to become the person you *think* they want to speak to. It's like writing a cover letter for a job that you want: you try to figure out what would be the most appropriate and polite way to communicate how you're the best person for the position, without saying anything that could potentially lose you the opportunity.

But when I changed the email's subject and body, we were being ourselves. We put ourselves out there, inviting interested parties to come take a look, and trusting that they would contact us if they liked what they saw. We weren't pitching, and we weren't trying to anticipate what they would want to hear.

BE YOURSELF SO YOUR PERFECT CLIENTS CAN FIND YOU.

I've had to learn this lesson many times. While I embraced it on Craigslist, I forgot it as soon as I changed marketing strategies. (Nobody on Craigslist pays very well, so it wasn't a stable business building strategy.)

In my quest for clients I discovered the world of networking. The idea is simple: join a group, meet with your fellow networkers often, and stay top of mind so you can send each other business.

I did this for more than a year, and completely burned out on it. In fact, I networked myself into debt because I spent all my time networking.

In retrospect, networking didn't work for me because I was in a *selling mindset*. I was desperately looking for clients for myself and as referrals for my colleagues. I would have taken any client who was willing to pay me. Again, think of it as dating! It's important to be yourself so the perfect person can find you (I was not), and desperation is a huge turnoff—in finding both a client and a significant other.

Everything changed when I evolved my pitch to reflect a noticeable, memorable, shareable brand and niche. I went into an *anti-selling mindset*. I was enthusiastically sharing my company with everyone I met, and I had zero attachment to closing them as clients. I actually *didn't want* to convince them; I wanted to engage *only* with people who were energized by my brand. *Those were my ideal clients!*

And what happened next was incredible: I

successfully networked myself out of networking.

I just didn't need to do it anymore. Once all the people I had previously met through networking heard about what we were selling and how, they started sending me ideal clients. I didn't need to interface with them regularly because I was already top of mind. I planted the seed of my brand in their consciousness, and that was much more powerful than all the networking meetings and coffee dates I had dragged myself to.

I was putting my energy into fully being my brand, owning our niche, and expressing it in everything I did. I stopped dressing in the so-called appropriate business casual clothing of the networking scene and started wearing my jeans and boots again. I stopped trying to be who I *thought* I needed to be to get the business, and started focusing on the value I had to offer.

And I realized, *once again*, that I had to be myself so my perfect clients could find me.

Most solopreneurs are too scared to be themselves. Because they need business, they are always trying to do what they *think* they need to do to get business.

But that's a selling mindset. Refocusing on finding your voice and your specialty is 10 times more powerful for building a steady stream of top-tier clients.

Once I fully embraced the anti-selling mindset, networking didn't seem like a good use of my time.

Instead, I got to work building my brand's value and reputation. I started writing useful articles on my blog, sharing knowledge that I thought would both benefit my market and demonstrate my expertise.

Despite stage fright, I forced myself to start giving talks. Because why spend an hour demonstrating your expertise to *one* person when you could use the same amount of time talking to a *room full of people*—and be seen as even more of an expert merely because you're onstage?

Again, I was not in a selling mindset in any of these contexts. Instead I put my energy into sharing valuable information—and it was freeing. I could share what I know about branding and it would naturally attract my ideal clients—who were already fans and didn't need to be convinced to buy.

When I was networking, I was constantly trying to prove that we were great designers and nice people to work with. And even when I *did* get referrals, I experienced a lot of ghosting: prospective clients who suddenly disappear after we have had many conversations and submitted a proposal.

As a friend of mine once told me when I was a flailing real estate agent: *Desperation is a stinky cologne.*

And that's why working in sales sucks—and I, like many people, *hate sales.*

LESSON #3: HOW TO STOP SELLING

Let's get really clear on what I mean by sales. "Sales" is an icky word because it usually means someone is *trying to convince you* to buy from them. Most people hate selling because that is what they are doing: trying to convince someone to buy their product. So when I refer to "selling" versus "not selling," I'm referring to a way of thinking that will influence everything you say, do, and write.

A "selling mindset" is invested in closing the deal, willing to sell to anyone willing to pay, hoping to sell to as many people as possible. You are trying to convince someone that you are the best option.

An "anti-selling mindset" is the opposite. It's about *being yourself* and shouting who you are, what you do, and how you do it from the rooftops—all the time. Instead of trying to be the person you think will get the sale, employing sales tactics and sales pipeline strategies, you're focused on being the best version of yourself and your business so you *attract the right kind of clients*; the ones who will truly value and appreciate your efforts.

Think about how those two conversations feel when you're on the receiving end. The first is telling you all the reasons you should buy something, and has a rebuttal for any resistance. It doesn't feel like the person doing it cares about you, does it? The second, however, is asking you about your needs, and then exploring how their service may or *may not* be a good fit.

Which do you prefer?

Let's look at a common sales process: intro call, follow-up call(s), pitching, lots of talking, unpaid proposals that take a lot of time, maybe some schmoozing, and then, often, radio silence. After spending all that time, clients often fall silent after the proposal stage because they are too embarrassed to tell you that they don't want to hire you.

There is nothing fun about this process. Yet most entrepreneurs I meet endure this cycle over and over again—because it's the only way they know how to do it.

That's why I teach how *not to sell,* which requires a complete shift in mindset and intention.

BADASS BRANDS DON'T SELL.

When you have a Badass Brand, you turn into a detective. You are looking for your perfect clients, and *only* your perfect clients. Some sales-training courses teach tactics like "push people away to attract them to the sale." They know that often people want what they can't have.

While this Badass Brand technique looks similar, it's actually the opposite because the goal and intention are different. Badass Brands are genuinely not trying to sell their services to a prospect because they *don't want a client who isn't perfect for them.*

Basically, Badasses don't want to work with weak clients.

When you are genuinely looking for a specific kind of client, and not just anyone who will buy, your interaction with people completely shifts from selling to not selling.

When you make this shift, an amazing thing happens. You start to *build a reputation that precedes you.* You elevate yourself to expert status with everyone you speak to. You demonstrate that you know your value and don't settle for less. You show your integrity and build trust with everyone you meet.

This comes when you have a very clear understanding and confidence of your value in the world. And when you have that confidence, you understand the opportunity cost of working with clients who aren't ideal and you are genuinely not interested in working with them. You are confident that a better client is always right around the corner.

CASE STUDY: KRISTINA, SAT & ACT PREP TUTOR

Kristina Semos started her test-prep company out of necessity. A singer and performer with mathlete tendencies, she took a side gig as an SAT and ACT prep tutor when she lost her finance job during the recession. After a few years, she realized she could make more money tutoring on her own than working for a company.

And she did really well. She charged $170 to $200 per hour providing test prep to wealthy kids who wanted to get into top-notch colleges and needed the scores to compete.

On the one hand, she had a full schedule and got all of her clients through referrals. On the other hand, however, she had a really full schedule! Most days she raced around the city until 10 p.m., going from appointment to appointment, and she was exhausted. Plus, she felt she had hit her price ceiling, and was getting pushback for trying to increase it to more than the generally accepted rates in Manhattan.

Kristina also agreed to work with anyone, as long as they were willing to pay her rate. And she loved some clients, but some...not so much. (Elite NYC parents can be a tricky bunch.) She had naturally built a reputation as a trusted expert in her field, but her methods had hit their limit in terms of price.

By rebranding as Ivy Lounge Test Prep™, we completely shifted her positioning in the market to elite and expert. Instead of selling to anyone who would pay her rate, she was looking for a very specific type of client who wanted her method and level of expertise, and was willing not only to work on her new terms (travel to her office, have Skype sessions, self-schedule via an app), but also pay a higher rate to get it.

We developed a product called the Ace the Test Game Plan™, an introductory session much like her initial consultations, but with more process and structure. During these sessions, she would interview students, analyze their test scores thus far, and discuss their goals and habits. Then she would provide a write-up of her findings with a testing timeline, determine whether to take the SAT or ACT, target scores, and suggestions of how to achieve their goals. We priced it at $750.

This is the first step in *not* selling. During a quick phone call, Kristina asks questions about the student, then explains the process. This process, and its price, will not work for everyone. Some people are just looking to hire someone for hourly work at their home, and those aren't her clients.

By using the Ace the Test Game Plan™, both parties are able to experience what it is like to work together. There is no pitching. Kristina doesn't want to convince someone to hire her if they don't feel like they've gotten tremendous value from this initial engagement. Those who purchase an Ace the Test Game Plan™ experience how brilliant she is in the field. Based on the results, she recommends a solution for the student: a package suitable for their specific situation and goals.

After reviewing the Game Plan, the potential client can sign up for the full tutoring package—but Kristina doesn't want or need to sell. She is offering a service, but she is detached from the outcome. The potential client is not a good fit for her services if they don't want to pay for it. If they want to just hire her hourly, at their home, outside her hours of availability, then they aren't respecting the expertise she brings to the table.

Kristina knows there are more clients right around the corner. As her business continues to develop, she receives referrals who have heard about and want her Ace the Test Game Plan™. It's a clear, valuable, and distinct offer that makes it easy to talk about and easy to trust. It's also an easy buy-in for her target market— the individuals who can do a Game Plan with her and get results right away, and then decide to move forward with a tutoring package.

About a month after we rebranded Ivy Lounge Test Prep™, Kristina emailed me, excited to report that she had closed two Game Plans in one day. The following week she forwarded me the receipt from her first client: a charge for $9,200 directly into her bank account.

She said when she calculated it out, she was making almost $700 per session, and that number will actually increase as she closes more clients.

Now *that* is Badass.

SHAKE YOUR BADASS

To get in the anti-selling mindset, you need to focus on communicating your unique value to everyone you meet—and trust that you are going to continuously attract an unlimited number of clients by being noticeable, memorable, and shareable.

So instead of trying to say what might be correct, or using so-called sales tactics, think about this: Whether you are meeting someone for coffee, speaking on stage, or writing an article on your blog, what do you want your audience to take away from the exchange? I call this the "one thing."

- What's the *one thing* you want someone to remember about you after you leave?
- Is it different than what your competitors want them to remember?
- What qualities do you look for in an ideal client?
- How would you determine if someone is a *perfect* fit for you? Write a list of questions you would ask potential clients to figure out if they are right for you.

WHAT SELLING ART ON THE STREET TAUGHT ME ABOUT BADASS BRANDING

The first summer Steve and I were together, we were hustling to make ends meet. I was trying to close rental deals as a new real estate agent in the crappy 2009 economy and subsidizing my income with a couple of nights bartending. Steve was applying for agency jobs every day with little luck, and doing cheap design gigs off Craigslist when available.

Even living with my friend in a rent-controlled apartment with low rent, it was hard to stay afloat in Manhattan. When it became clear that Steve was not necessarily going to land a gig anytime soon, he said he was probably going to have to apply for some unrelated job, like stocking clothes at H&M for minimum wage.

But I just couldn't let that happen. Here was this incredibly talented guy whose art I had fallen in love with even before I fell in love with him, and he was going to work in an unrelated field for minimum wage? What a waste! I saw a huge opportunity.

I told him we were going to sell his art instead. I didn't know how, but I knew that because I loved it so much we could find a way to make money.

So we took to the streets like many artists we had seen. One Saturday afternoon, we packed up a bunch of ink drawings and a table and headed to Union Square.

Well, we learned the ways of the street art scene pretty quickly. The buyers in Union Square are predominantly tourists, and tourists want souvenirs; they don't want to spend a lot. The pieces that sold the best had iconic NYC images in them: the Brooklyn Bridge, the Empire State Building, the Chrysler Building.

So I encouraged him to paint the classics, and while he wasn't exactly inspired to do so, he did it—because we needed to sell these paintings to live!

We couldn't figure out why, but it didn't go as planned. Steve tried to re-create the paintings that previously sold, but the replicas just never seemed to get the same kind of action. It was almost like the magic was sucked out of the art, and the buyers could tell these pieces were craft and not an artist's inspired piece.

We had switched to a selling mindset, and the buyers could tell the difference.

Years later, we learned how important the art of not selling is. Instead, Steve paints his own visions of exactly what he wants. He is committed to his authentic vision for his art, and it has allowed him to build his own Badass Art Brand: stevewasterval.com.

CHAPTER FOUR

THE FORMULA OF BADASSERY

Once Steve and I focused on our niche and our process, our pipeline started filling itself with hungry clients. When you have more client demand than time to service them, you can do one of two things: hire staff to help you out, or raise your price.

We chose the latter. After failing miserably with staff, we were relishing in our newfound freedom from payroll. And with some lingering PTSD from the debt, we weren't looking to repeat history.

So we started raising our prices each month, while we simultaneously refined our process and increased the value of our offerings. And just like before, we started pricing ourselves out of a lot of our biggest fans.

We had originally built the Brandup to help small

businesses with a lower-priced service of $3,000. At $10,000, it was no longer accessible to a group of people that really needed it.

And that was a major reason we decided to build an online course called The Brandup Bootcamp. While we could no longer sell our time and services for $3,000 per day, we could use our process and practical know-how to walk solopreneurs through the steps of building their own Badass Brand according to our philosophy.

This was an incredible experience. Not only did we learn all kinds of things about online courses, online marketing, and video creation, but it also forced us to articulate a lot of strategies we knew inherently that we had been implementing for clients for years, but had never expressed outright.

It also forced us to take a close look at how we approached the process of branding businesses. We dissected what made our company stand out in the market, and investigated what we did to help each client stand out in its industry. We discovered that there are four fundamental opportunities to set yourself apart from the competition. And the intersection of at least two is critical for building a Badass Brand.

In order to create a DIY Bootcamp that entrepreneurs could use to build their own Badass Brands, we developed those four distinct methods into a concrete and tangible formula. Any small service business can use this formula to uncover its own Badassery, and to use as a benchmark to determine if you already have the foundation of a Badass Brand.

This formula always works because it capitalizes on the advantages small businesses have over their larger competitors. Even though you may not have a lot of resources or staff to help get your brand out there, you need only a small group of high-paying clients to do very well for yourself. By narrowing in on a clear niche, you immediately position yourself as an expert, and can command a premium price.

LESSON #4: THE 4 ANGLES OF BADASSERY

Here's how it works: There are four potential angles, but you need at least two in order to qualify as a Badass Brand. Committing to a minimum of two is critical to your success.

If you can get three or four angles, even better! Some businesses aren't necessarily capable of having all four angles because of their industry, and that's okay. But when possible, the more the better.

Keep in mind your responses to questions in the previous chapters while you read this. Use your favorite and most profitable clients as a starting point for developing your angles. Don't pick areas of focus that don't match up to what you love to do; if you go through this process and end up with a business you're barely excited to run, it doesn't get the BADASS stamp of approval.

ANGLE 1: TARGET MARKET

This is the most obvious angle, and I'm sure you've heard it before: Identify your target market. These are the people you are trying to sell your services to. But I have a twist.

Everyone has some kind of target market, but just any target doesn't suffice when it comes to The 4 Angles Formula. For your target market to count, it must be specific enough that your ideal clients would hear about your business and self-identify as your perfect client.

For example, targeting women is not specific enough. Although as a woman, I can see that this is geared toward women, nothing about it tells me I am specifically the ideal customer. But women between the ages of 25 and 40 who do yoga? That's specific and allows people to clearly self-identify as your ideal client (or not). My ears would perk up if I heard that, because I fall into that category—and I would think this business might actually interest me.

A specific target market is usually defined as a

combination of a few of the following: age, gender, family status, hobby/interest, industry, job, business, life milestone, kind of company, or size of company. The more specific you can be, the better.

The decision on where to narrow should not be arbitrary. You want to base it on previous experiences, ideally who you enjoy and who is most profitable to work with. It's okay if you can't narrow down because you haven't had enough experience to make the decision. And if you feel stuck and can't comfortably narrow, then you don't have to use this as one of your angles!

Here's an example of hyper-focusing based on previous experiences: I had a client who worked in mindset coaching, specifically around money. When she came to us, she had been doing life coaching for all sorts of people, even though she generally attracted women. But her personal story and enthusiasm became apparent when she was helping single moms like herself figure out their money issues. Specifically, and this was very authentic to her voice, Single Mom Money Shit.

All single moms have to deal with financial issues, whether they have very little money or a lot of it . They also deal with a lot of contradictory feelings about how they can and should spend their money that other people might not.

This client had personal experience with these issues. She is so real and relatable to these women in particular that by owning the intersection of single moms and money issues, she could immediately position herself in the market as something new and different.

I won't lie: this was hard for her. A lot of other advisors claimed that her approach was too narrow and urged her to, at the very least, focus on money issues for women.

However, I can think of five or six coaches off the top of my head—just in my network—who focus on money mindset for women. And then there is Suze Orman, who is known internationally for it! But can you think of anyone who is known for helping single moms with their money mindset issues?

Single moms have a unique set of issues to deal with, and this client can be a much more effective coach to other single moms because she has been there, so she can relate. Single moms, in turn, will be more attracted to her because they will believe she knows what they are going through—and that she'll be able to adequately address their needs in a way that other coaches can't.

Finally, if you were a single mom, wouldn't you be

much more interested in working with her instead of other money mindset coaches for women? Working with a money mindset coach might sound expensive, but someone who works with women *just like you* with your *exact* challenges becomes much more attractive.

Self-identifying as the ideal client lowers the barrier to entry.

To recap: Angle 1 is about a narrow target market, and needs to be highly specific for this to count as one of your minimum two angles. If you can't get specific enough, that's okay; it just doesn't count toward one of your two angles. Fortunately, there are three others to choose from.

ANGLE 2: PERSONALITY

What's the brand personality, or voice, that will stand out in the crowd? This is what many people think of when they think of a brand.

Developing a Badass Brand personality helps make all business decisions easier in the future. When you are clear on your personality, choosing design is easier. Deciding what to write about on your blog becomes clearer, as does the language you use. Even making decisions on where to market becomes easier.

Why?

Because now you can step outside yourself and

your personal tastes and preferences and make decisions in the third person. It's no longer my business; it's Worstofall Design. When we look at a marketing opportunity—say, a sponsorship at an event—we ask ourselves, "*Is this something Worstofall Design would attend? Does the brand of the event fit with Worstofall Design's personality?*"

Your brand will have a distinct brand personality regardless of whether you deliberately build one. But without intention or thought, you'll end up with either a very generic me-too brand personality or, even worse, a completely bland, forgettable personality. Often, they are one and the same.

And sometimes that's okay, or even necessary. But for your brand personality to count as one of your four angles, it must meet this requirement: *It must somehow be contrary or in contrast to the prevailing personality in your industry.*

As with Angle 1, when using our four angles formula, you don't have to buck the status quo and be different in order to have a Badass Brand. And I wouldn't want you to make up something *just* to be different; that's inauthentic, and not the goal.

Instead, you want to apply Angle 2 when there is something authentic to you and your approach to business that *is* distinct within your industry.

Once you find that, it's your job to *own it.* And be extreme about it. Blow it up and put it all over your website. Dare to be different from your competitors. Dare to be disliked by your competitors or potential customers.

Sound scary? It can be. You are blazing new territory, and some people aren't going to like it, get it, or support it.

That's why we say Badass Brands require guts—because being loved by some means being misunderstood, and even disliked, by others.

But that's the opportunity. If it's authentic to you—if you are doing it with the goal of being excellent at what you do—then you will attract a loyal following of ideal clients who relate to and appreciate your authentic voice and approach.

But it *must* be authentic to you, and it must be different from the general population to count toward your angles.

Stash Wealth—the financial services client whose story we told at the end of Chapter 2—is a perfect example of this. Their experience at Merrill Lynch made them accustomed to that corporate feel. Even though they set out to create a version of Merrill for a younger market, they got stuck making it inside the corporate box. They were designing a hipper Merrill Lynch instead of doing their own thing.

Only when we asked, "What are you against?" did they admit they were against everything that Merrill did, and it allowed them to start embracing their voice with enthusiasm. This voice contrasted their industry: young, hip, and sassy—very different from the corporate Wall Street voice of their competitors.

Now they send out summer cocktail recipes in their newsletters, make references to Taylor Swift, and even (gasp!) curse. Priya can often be found in ripped jeans and a blazer meeting with clients over craft beer.

None of that is okay in the Merrill Lynch world. Plenty of it makes sense in, for example, the ad agency world; if they were an ad agency with that kind of voice, I wouldn't count it as an Angle 2 because it would be the same as their competitors. But it does count as an Angle 2 in finance, because it is contrary to their industry. And that's why it's so Badass.

In sum: Your brand personality is relative to your competitors and industry. And it only counts if it is in contrast to the prevailing personality of your industry.

ANGLE 3: LEAD PRODUCT & SALES PROCESS

A sales process is a series of steps that turns leads into clients. Our approach to the sales process is different because it shortens the time from lead to sale, and eliminates the steps in between.

We've excluded all the free work that people usually do between meeting prospective clients and closing them and getting an initial payment. Instead, I take the first step of your process, productize it, and sell it for a relatively low price.

I call this building a lead product. It has the potential to completely transform the way you talk about your business, and how you sell. And it has many benefits.

First, a lead product makes it very clear to all interested buyers what the first step is to working with you. Instead of long, drawn-out conversations and time-consuming proposals (which you write for free), you prompt all potential clients to buy this lead product.

This saves tons of time. It turns the sales process (which I categorize as free work) into one short conversation. You get paid to develop a thoughtful proposal that also works to elevate your credibility in the mind of the consumer.

Second, lead products make you easy to talk about and share with colleagues, which creates an organic sales force. Prowess, a marketing consulting company that coaches fitness businesses, offers a Prowess Brand Boost™ as its lead product. The Brand Boost makes it easy for past clients to tell their fitness friends about Prowess because the Brand Boost is a tangible, valuable offering; it's easier to suggest than just referring a great marketing company. Everyone who does a Brand Boost is primed to hire Prowess for the full package, but the Brand Boost keeps customers coming in the door and telling their friends.

Having a lead product is like educating your fans on something simple and interesting to say about you.

Third, lead products take the pressure off the conversation for both parties. Whenever money exchanges hands, each side has different expectations. The client expects to get value, and can let down their guard because they aren't being sold to. The expert can focus on delivering value without the pressure of turning this free work into a paying client (and feeling like they wasted their time if the client doesn't sign).

Fourth, lead products demonstrate that your time and expertise are valuable, even during the evaluation phase. Your proposal will be better than anyone else's because you had paid time to work on it. And because the client paid for it, they will value the advice more highly than the free work they got from competitors. When you give your services away, you undermine your own value and credibility. People don't value free things. A paying client sets itself up to listen and trust more—which sets you up for success.

Finally, those that buy this smaller lead product are

buying into *you*. Once they've made that commitment psychologically, they are much more likely to hire you for the full project.

I know what you're thinking: Sometimes people or companies need a proposal. Maybe they are doing an RFP (Request for Proposal) and require them from multiple sources to make a comparison and come to a decision.

My instinct? Run the other way. These clients are time-wasters and usually end up being pretty unprofitable. And you'd be surprised what holding your ground and sticking to your no-proposal process can do. I was contacted for an RFP and relayed that we don't write proposals and that our first step is the Brandshrink. Six months later—presumably after a painful RFP process—that client came back and hired us, no questions asked.

But if those are the kind of clients you want, you're welcome to do the proposals for free. You just can't count Angle 3 as one of your angles.

Note: I would almost never suggest doing things like this for free; it weakens the brand's reputation, and cuts into your company's profitability. Badass Brands don't like to work with people that want free work. They value their services too highly and would rather work with fewer people at a high rate—people that pay for value. They know what they're worth, and don't like wasting time with those that don't.

It can be scary at first, but that's what makes it a Badass Brand, not a sissy brand.

Making a lead product is easy if you follow this formula.

1.   **It must be the first thing you do with a client.** Usually it has some form of intake or discovery. It's imperative that the client feels they're being heard during this process and that you understand them. A common mistake is to lecture the client in an attempt to show your knowledge. Don't do this. Use the time to listen and demonstrate your expertise with thoughtful questions.

2.   **It must have a valuable deliverable at the end, and work as a standalone product.** In other words, a client should be able to buy and get value out of this piece of your offering—even if they don't move forward.

3.   **Your lead product must solve a problem for the client—a problem they know they have.** A common mistake is to build a lead product that sells a problem, not a solution to a problem, like an audit or an assessment.

4.   **It must be a fixed price, with a fixed process.**

5.   **It must be branded.** That is, it must have a name, and not just a generic strategy session or

website audit or VIP day or something else that any of your competitors could also offer. Name it something unique so no other company can legally rip it off.

If you don't hit all of the points above, your lead product either will be hard to sell or won't help you close the clients you want.

For example, we worked with a speaking/communications/life coach who knows—after years of working with clients—that these skills actually change people's entire lives. This coach wanted to sell that transformational experience.

But the world is saturated with life coaches selling transformation. It's a hard sell because it has become generic, and it's also much harder to identify people looking for transformational help.

On the other hand, one of his specialties is speaker training, and tons of people know they want to be better public speakers.

That's a problem they *know they have*. So a great lead product for him is a two-hour training for people who want to present better. They get a personal evaluation and specific, actionable tips on how to improve their speaking skills moving forward.

At the very least, they leave the session with a heightened awareness of what they need to do to improve their speaking skills. But most people also leave with a greater understanding of how these skills will help them in all areas of their life.

The lead product gets clients in the door by selling something they know they need, and then allows them to experience all the benefits they could gain from working with *you*.

As experts, we know a lot more than our clients (that's why they are hiring us!). But many experts mistakenly try to *explain* why they are experts. This is too hard and too much work. It's much easier and more powerful to have the client *experience* your expertise firsthand. In other words, show, don't tell.

Imagine if you could either (1) read 20 testimonials of a life coach transforming people's lives or (2) speak with that coach for 15 minutes and have a breakthrough. Which scenario is more likely to get the sale?

Lead products allow you to get paid to demonstrate your greatness. That unique experience puts you in a *category of one* in the mind of the client who, until that point, has just been comparing company pitches, prices, and testimonials. Now that they have experienced your expertise, you suddenly become the only person who can solve their problem (after all, you've already solved part of it!).

This is one of the most exciting concepts I share

with entrepreneurs, because many people believe you have to give away your time in order to close a client. It sometimes necessitates a perceptual shift that requires you to—once again—truly believe in your expertise and the value you have to offer.

People buy from people they know, like, and trust, and selling someone a low-priced lead product allows you to cut the line. Spend a little time demonstrating your expertise, and they will jump from knowing to liking and trusting you much more quickly.

ANGLE 4: BULL'S EYE PRODUCT

If you can accomplish this, my friends, it will change your life.

This is what most of my branding questions help target: how to build a branded service with a unique process, which is specific to you and only you, for a flat fee. If you can design this, my advice is to sell *only* that. When done right, this Bull's Eye product is highly profitable *and* it's the thing you love most about your work.

Building a Bull's Eye product means developing a profitable business you love that sells easily and can organically become more profitable over time. The easy part is crucial here, because we are ultimately looking to build a business that creates freedom in your life—and hunting for clients are the shackles we need to break.

Every prospective client call made me nervous during the first few years of our business. Each situation had a new set of expectations, and because I wasn't yet adept at taking control of projects, the client dictated those expectations. They laid out exactly what they wanted, and I did whatever I could to accommodate their price and timeline. It's a delicate dance between trying to anticipate the time needed and trying to cover your ass from unforeseen hiccups. I didn't realize that because the client was calling the shots, they were also determining whether the project went smoothly.

I also wasn't aware that clients *don't know what they don't know*. Essentially, they are steering a ship without knowing how to drive, or even how the boat works. As a service provider, I was letting them steer that ship, and they would almost always go in the wrong direction.

This is where the Bull's Eye product comes in.

We went over the distinction between them in Chapter 2, but this product is what turns you from service provider into expert. Build a product based on your unique expertise; one that's specific and replicable. You become more proficient at your process through repetition, and because you get more information about what works and what doesn't, you can continuously improve.

As time goes on, your refined process elevates you higher and higher above the competition. Meanwhile, your competitors are spending their time customizing their process to each client, thereby taking the long road to expert. They too learn from every project, but because each one is so different, it takes a lot longer to get clear on what works and what doesn't.

The Bull's Eye product eliminates the guesswork and takes back control of each project. You're calling the shots because it's *your* process. You know how it works better than the client. When you complete a process over and over again, you have the experience and authority to guide the client every step of the way and explain how to produce the best results. And your ability to guide the client is worth the premium price you charge.

Let's take Ivy Lounge Test Prep™ as an example. SAT prep services are meant to help the student achieve their goals, but parents who foot the bill often feel entitled to dictate the process. Essentially, Kristina had both the students and the parents as clients, although she was charging only for the tutoring sessions with the students. She didn't have a process for the parents to engage, so her relationship with them was ad hoc, and she had to deal with frantic emails and phone calls.

This could also be detrimental to the students and their results. Kristina found that when parents participate too much, it hurts the student's confidence. And confidence is one critical way to boost a test score.

When Kristina allowed the parents to pay per session, students may not always have gotten the best results possible because there was no system to manage their overbearing parents. Kristina didn't see a way around that, given that the parents were paying the bill.

This changed when Ivy Lounge Test Prep™ developed a Bull's Eye product. Taking both student and parent needs into account, her best solution for clients was a combination of tutoring, weekly office hours, and parent check-ins to keep them informed on progress and give them a chance to ask questions. By controlling the process, Ivy Lounge was anticipating parents' needs and making them feel heard. However, it also ensured that Kristina would manage this involvement so it wouldn't have a negative effect on the student's ability to achieve—and she received appropriate payment for that extra time. This process also elevated Ivy Lounge to expert consultant status, so Kristina is now able to charge more than her competitors, and deliver more value by getting better results.

Ivy Lounge gets higher test scores because they take charge by guiding a client who doesn't know any better. Even though it can be scary to say no to the person paying you, the best clients will respect you for knowing your stuff. In fact, they realize that they are paying you *because* you know more about said topic—and you would actually be doing them a disservice if you didn't say no.

Clients who don't like that aren't good clients for you. Either they will take up your time unnecessarily, or they just won't be satisfied—and won't be a good referral source. Either way, your time is better spent finding the next client.

THIS IS HOW WORSTOFALL DESIGN TARGETS THE FOUR ANGLES:

Angle 1, Target Market: We work only with one- to three-person service businesses.

Angle 2, Brand Personality: We have a contrarian attitude. From our name to our brand voice in our articles and materials, we swim against the current.

Angle 3, Lead Product: We sell the Brandshrink as the first step to anyone interested in working with us; we don't do proposals or pitch in any way.

Angle 4, Bull's Eye Product: We work only in Brandups, our signature one- to two- day brand-building intensive. We don't do custom projects.

MINI CASE STUDIES

I share three mini case studies because, as I mentioned, not all companies can manage to hit all four angles. Two angles can be enough—so let's see how that works.

KATHLEEN, SAVVY OFFICE SYSTEMS

Kathleen is a professional organizer who originally worked with individuals and small businesses. After answering the Brandshrink questions, she decided to focus on organizing offices and systems for small businesses because she enjoyed them more and they were more profitable. Not only do businesses tend to value professional services more, but they also stand to see a return on their investment in a way that people organizing their home usually can't (although I can assure you individuals also get a major return, but it may not be financial). This focus counts as Angle 1 (although if I were being a hardass I'd like it to be a little more specific).

Then she created a lead product called the Game Plan Express (Angle 3), which she describes as "for the motivated DIYer to get your office in order." In a 90-minute virtual meeting, she will look at your situation and give you a plan to get organized. Once you see what she can do, you'll probably want her help doing it!

And when you do, she has a great Bull's Eye product to sell you (Angle 4). Now, I love this example because a Bull's Eye product doesn't have to be so fancy or different; it's anything you love to do in a set process.

Her main Bull's Eye product is performing a full-day, in-person office reorganization, as well as developing systems to keep that office clutter-free. In true Bull's Eye form, this is what most people need and should buy. It solves their immediate problem and also addresses the maintenance piece. Although most people want the cleanup, they don't necessarily feel the need for the systems part because they don't understand what that looks like. But this solution provides the *highest, longest-lasting value*, so this is what Kathleen recommends to most clients (when they need it, of course!).

Her downsell is the full-day declutter without the systems, and her upsell includes ongoing one-on-one support to work on additional systems and make sure the ones she developed are being used.

In the first seven weeks after launching these productized services she sold one of each, totaling $10,000. And that was just the beginning. A few months later, she told me she had raised her prices because she was selling so easily—without any of the sales friction and anxiety she used to have. And she was getting such great feedback on how valuable her work was that she was confident she could charge even more in the future!

LAURA, DIVORCE COACH

Laura Bonarrigo had a successful career as a soap opera star on *One Life to Live*. But when she walked in our doors, it was clear that her passion and focus had grown bigger.

While going through a long and painful second divorce (third, if you count her parents'), Laura sought support. After becoming a Certified Life Coach and Certified Divorce Coach, she found her calling: she wanted to do something positive with her experiences and concentrate on helping those with broken hearts.

Laura is an eloquent, intelligent, fierce woman, and because of her career as an actress, she presents very well. When I asked what she disliked about her industry, she said it all looks the same. Coaches, especially divorce coaches, tend to have a touchy-feely personality to their brand. They sugarcoat their message, handling clients like delicate flowers.

That isn't real, from Laura's point of view. Divorce is hard and people get nasty. And Laura is not one to beat around the bush.

During the Brandshrink interview I took down her words verbatim as she went on a tear about the challenges of divorce.

"Can I get real? Going through any heartache, especially divorce, stinks. It's usually really, really difficult…I call this kind of pain a modern-day rite of passage because it's one of those things that forces you to wake up and say good-bye to a life that isn't working. Good morning, sunshine!"

When I told her we should publish these raw feelings on her site, she laughed nervously. "Isn't that going to offend people?" she asked. "Can I really say that?"

To which I said yes, of course you can say that on your website. This is a great example of Angle 2: owning a voice and a style of speaking and writing that goes against the prevailing personality in your industry. If that's who you are, that's the fire that is going to attract your ideal clients—because it's the very approach they're seeking. And those who don't like it? Not your clients.

Not everyone is going to like the casual and frank way Laura speaks, because they are looking for a touchy-feely coach. Those people won't hire her anyway. She was much better off expressing her true voice and connecting with people who would appreciate it and find it valuable.

I told Laura to embrace her voice, and to talk about the parts of divorce others won't touch. Talk about sex.

Talk about anger. Talk about dating after divorce. Talk about what really goes through your mind. Let it out. It will resonate with your people, and that's what a Badass Brand does.

Laura offers her fans—the ones who love what she's saying and contact her to see how she works—a lead product called Divorce Unloaded™ (Angle 3). This initial session allows Laura to get to know the client, help them understand mental blocks in their way, explain where they are doing things right, give them a plan, and assess whether they could benefit from her work.

This puts her in a great position to suggest what's in the client's best interest—which doesn't mean trying to sell her service to everyone. She has told some clients that they don't need her, even though they want to pay her, because she doesn't want to work with people who aren't going to get results.

We're so proud of Laura for being brave enough to take this approach. She was nervous, but immediately started to see results. People loved her voice and loved reading her words. She started getting invited to speak at events as a Divorce Coach. What she had to say was real, raw, and engaging. It was authentic. (A grossly overused word, but it's true.)

And she also positioned herself as an expert who gets paid for her advice instead of giving free sessions, which allowed her to charge more right out of the gate.

She puts herself out there and allows herself to be vulnerable, and that's what people respond to.

It takes guts; that's why Laura is a bona fide Badass.

JOHN, PHOTOGRAPHER

Photographers, like many people in creative fields, often believe their work speaks for itself. That's why most of their websites are mainly portfolios full of images and categories representing what they do.

When we met John DeMato, he offered photography in all areas. He did events, portraits, headshots, and video. As he explained it, whatever people needed, he would do—he had to keep the lights on!

After he worked one of our events I hired him to do my headshots. But I knew I wanted more: I'm positioning myself as an expert in my field, so I not only wanted a headshot but also needed lifestyle photos I could use on marketing material, in ads, and on my website. I needed variety, and I wanted access to as many photos as I could get.

In my experience, most photographers don't want to give you access to their photos. Instead, they provide a select set to maintain quality control over their work (and because the photos are valuable). This frustrates me. Especially as a branding company, I want a stable of photos to use, and because we can edit images in-house there is no extra work for the photographer.

I laid it out, and we agreed on a price, hired hair and makeup, and set a date. Steve and I came up with a shot list and outfits that were in line with my brand. When John showed up, we were ready to rock!

It was an intense day. I changed clothes more than a dozen times. John took thousands of photos, and the results were incredible. I have always been camera shy, but John was skilled at getting the natural look out of me. By the end of the shoot I was actually having fun, and you could see it in the pictures.

It became clear to all of us that John was sitting on a gold mine. The world of experts and thought leaders is growing, and they all need content that makes them look like the Badasses they are. And they will pay for it!

After months of hearing my pitch for narrowing, John was finally convinced. We helped him focus his offerings on thought leaders (Angle 1) and packaged services (Angle 4) into three levels of shoots that these business owners need. When you work with John you learn that he has a lot of Angle 2 in him as well. His personality and how he communicates with the subject is incredibly unique, which comes through from the moment you first get on the phone with him.

I love John's story because when I met him, he was

highly against narrowing. And nine months later—well, I'll let him tell you:

"*Rebranding was the best move I made for my business. I have never been this laser focused and in tune with my ideal clients' pain points. In fact, I never thought that I would have to have an ideal client—I mean, whoever pays me is my ideal client, right? WRONG! By carving out this high-end niche, I've increased my reach to well-paying and awesome clients who value my work like no other, and I've simultaneously separated myself from the jack-of-all-trades, master-of-none photographers fighting and clawing over discount-shopper clients who want something for nothing.*

As I continue to build the foundation for my business (content, promotion, etc.), I know that I will very soon become the go-to lifestyle portrait photographer for high-level entrepreneurs and thought leaders, mostly because my clients keep repeating this to me! Not only am I presenting myself as an expert, but I also believe I am an expert, and this positive attitude has reverberated through every aspect of my business and my personal life.

As for revenue overall, the $9,000 from three clients in the first month of the year is about $8,000 more than the same time period last year. I haven't even cold emailed anyone yet, but you did say that at the *beginning my revenue would come from referrals of those who advocate on my behalf :).*"

I got chills when John emailed this to me, and I hope it inspires you to take the leap. He was scared at first and he didn't believe it. But once he crossed over it didn't just have an almost-instant effect on his profit, it also changed his entire relationship with his business!

SHAKE YOUR BADASS

Fill out the 4 angles matrix on the next page (or better yet, use the workbook available at badassyourbrand. com/workbook). Brainstorm right now any and all possible angle opportunities. Don't limit yourself to what you think is doable, just start by imagining what's possible. You can decide later which parts you're going to take action on.

ANGLE #1: TARGET MARKET

**ANGLE #3: LEAD PRODUCT/
SALES PROCESS**

ANGLE #2: BIG PERSONALITY

ANGLE #4: BULL'S EYE PRODUCT

WHAT INHERITING THE NAME "Worstofall Design" TAUGHT ME ABOUT BADASS BRANDING

When we first started, a great deal of people told us not to use the name Worstofall Design. They said things like, "You don't want to lead with a negative in business." "People might think you do bad work." "You are going to confuse people or turn them off."

But we've found that standing out has little to do with being "right" or "good" or following the rules—and much more to do with getting noticed and building a lasting, memorable reputation, and accentuating what's different about you. It's hard for potential clients to measure how good you are without working with you, but if you have a couple of great angles, that's what people notice first. That's what draws them in.

The name Worstofall Design is our company doubling down on our Angle 2—our contrarian personality. It isn't enough to say you're different; you have to be different. Our name lets you know we aren't afraid to stand out. The name exemplifies a cornerstone of our philosophy: you must walk the walk.

And while other companies will tell you to do things differently, to varying degrees, we're saying, *Push it further. Go extreme on something. Exaggerate how you do things, how you talk, or who you work with. Whatever it is, make sure you do it enough to really*

hang your reputation on—and for people to notice and
remember you.

When people ask why we chose the name Worstofall, I say, "Because we build Badass Brands, and that's the most Badass name of all!" And that's how I emphasize our brand voice. If I said it was a play on our last name—Wasterval—that just wouldn't have as much gravitas.

When thinking about your angles, explore how, whenever possible, you can *be* your brand's angles through your actions, rather than just expressing them in words. Simply talking about your brand merely results in most people saying the same thing.

We chose not to go with "we help companies build a brand that dares to be different" on our homepage because we chose not to be lame. Our homepage copy now reads, "Badass Brands require guts, because being loved by some means being misunderstood, and even disliked, by others. They stand against something as much as they stand for something. Badass Brands are brave, sometimes irreverent, and always unapologetic, and for it they gain a kind of loyal following that can't be bought, only earned." And while some people might not know what the hell we're talking about, our clients write me love notes about that paragraph.

"...but at least I'm my own boss."

CHAPTER FIVE

PRICED FOR FREEDOM

Our main goal when we started Worstofall Design was just to stay afloat financially without having to work anywhere else. We didn't care if we worked all the time, and we didn't care much about the quality of the projects. We knew we would be happy if we could just make enough money to avoid going back to so-called regular jobs.

In other words, we were happy to take what we could get.

We had set a pretty low bar for ourselves, which probably led to us being overworked and underpaid longer than necessary. We defined our benchmark for success as, literally, just getting by. There was no quality of life built into our success plan. Nor was there any mention of the kind of work we wanted. We felt like we couldn't define the kinds of clients we wanted because we had never gotten clients, and we thought that beggars couldn't be choosers.

Three years after launching—when we were forced to reevaluate our business because we were in debt—we also had to ask ourselves what we were really going for.

What did our ideal situation look like?

What did success mean to us?

We realized we had some clear values on which to base our decisions:

- We value freedom over our time above all else. We work for ourselves because we don't want a boss—and that includes being slaves to our clients.

- We value self-development and learning. We wanted to be able to take time off for ourselves without worrying that our business would suffer—and use that time to explore other interests and business ideas.

- We value being energized by the work we do each day. We wanted to spend our time doing high-value work, and minimize the time we spent doing energy-draining low-value work. (I'd rather spend a day writing articles that inspire thousands of people than do my books, for which I can hire a bookkeeper.)

Once we defined these three pillars, it was much easier to decide to specialize in our intensive business model, where we don't do ongoing work with clients. We were also clear that the previous business model we had been using—the traditional agency model— was not going to get us the success we were looking for, no matter how successful we were!

Before we articulated our definition of success, we were striving for a default version of success based on higher and higher revenue. I mean, running business is about making money, right?

Sure it is. And if you're not making any, I'd call it more of a hobby than a business. But earning more and more money is open-ended. So if that's your goal, when will you ever feel successful?

If you want to be successful, feel successful, and reap the benefits of your success, you will get there faster and with less anxiety if you define what it means to you, and what it looks like when you get there.

Six months after we were $40,000 in debt, we pivoted our business and started attracting ideal clients because we were no longer a generic me-too brand selling "great design" like everyone else. We had achieved much of what we were looking for, which we knew because we had identified it beforehand.

We were no longer slaves to ongoing clients. We were energized by the work we were doing.

But we were also booked solid with multiple Brandups each week. We were making great money, and that can be addictive. But we knew we hadn't quite achieved what we were looking for—that freedom-over-our-time piece was still missing.

So we did what we knew we needed and booked a three-week off-the-grid trip to Maui. We weren't even that excited about it at the time; we loved the work we were doing and didn't want to rip our lives away (I know, cry me a river).

But we also know how these kinds of unplugged trips create the mental space needed to see big-picture ideas that move our lives in the direction we want. We knew it would allow us to step away from the hustle of making money and come up with long-term goals, plus strategies and plans for getting there.

We further honed our definition of success on this trip. We read and reread some of our favorite books. Three in particular—*Rich Dad Poor Dad*, *The Fountainhead*, and *The 4- Hour Workweek*—were foundational in the next evaluation of our definition of success.

We realized that we hadn't achieved one of our

core values: to create the time to spend on growing ourselves, our personal projects, and our other business ideas. So we dug deeper and got more granular on what it specifically meant to achieve these goals:

- Create space for Steve to move into painting as a full-time job, thereby building the #SELLOUT art brand.
- Build brand reputation and recognition to allow Pia to help more people find the financial and time freedom they want.

Both of the above required more time, which meant we needed to make more money working fewer hours. This is when we realized we had to systemize our Brandups in order to spend chunks of time making money and working with clients and free up chunks of time for other projects. This also meant we needed to price the Brandups accordingly.

We used our current expenses to determine that we needed to bring in $20,000 per month to continue living comfortably as we were, cover our taxes and business expenses, and still have a little left over for savings and unexpected expenses. This meant at roughly $10,000 per one-day Brandup, we could do one Brandup a week comfortably, take on two per month, and have the other two weeks a month to work on other projects. If we had inquiries for a third Brandup in a given month, we could decide to take it and stash the cash for a rainy day, or push it off because we knew we needed to invest our time in our other projects.

This decision clarified a lot. For one thing, we became very clear how many projects we needed on average each month, and created a lot of space for our other projects. After doing this for a few months, we learned we could also apply this formula to an entire year: We needed to do only 24 one-day Brandups annually, and we could space that out in whatever way worked best for us.

Once you realize that you need to work with clients only half the year, your sense of freedom—and opportunity to decide whether you want to make more money—increases dramatically.

LESSON #5: THE 50/25/25 RULE TO PROFIT & FREEDOM

When entrepreneurs proudly tell me they are overbooked with clients and either they haven't had to market or they have too much work to put time into their brand or website, I quietly chuckle to myself. I know it seems exciting to be overrun with clients, but all I hear is that you're not charging enough and you're working more than you need to for less money than you could be making.

I constantly preach the value of saying "no" so you can narrow and focus your expertise. But most businesses I've worked with consider saying no only after they have a pretty steady stream of referrals and potential clients filling up their email. However, there's another amazing thing you can and should do when this happens: raise your price.

What follows is a clear and concise way to develop your target pricing so you build a profitable business that also provides time to continue to build your value—and enjoy your life while you're at it. When you are selling several different services or products, there tends to be a lot of fancy math involved to understand your break-even point and profit margins. However, when you are a solopreneur—especially if you follow the Lead Product/Bull's Eye Product method—it doesn't have to be that complicated. In fact, as you narrow and focus, you can almost eliminate that math (or the guilt of not doing it) completely if you follow what I call the 50/25/25 Rule to Profit & Freedom™.

Would you rather have 50 clients paying $1,000 per project, or 10 clients paying $5,000?

Both scenarios yield $50,000. But in the first scenario, you're working for 50 clients, which leads to extra churn created by having to manage and service a large number of accounts. In the second scenario, you are merely looking to delight 10 ideal clients who understand your value—and are willing to pay more for it.

This smaller workload would leave you with extra time, so what do you do with it? You could get more business. Or you could take a break, relax, tackle a personal project, or work on your business, rather than in it.

If fewer higher-paying clients sounds like your speed, read on for my recipe for making it happen.

HOW TO IMPLEMENT THE 50/25/25 RULE TO PROFIT & FREEDOM

The goal when using this formula is to spend 50 percent of your time working for paying clients, 25 percent of your time building your brand and increasing your value, and 25 percent of your time any way you choose.

To integrate this method into your business strategy, we work backward from our goal revenue. First, figure out how much money you need to make annually to cover all your expenses and live comfortably.

If you need $120,000 a year, then your **Baseline Revenue Goal** is $10,000 per month. Using the 50/25/25 Rule, you know you want to make $10,000 per month spending 50 percent of your time on client work—or two weeks out of the month.

Next, determine how many clients you can take care of within that time frame. If you can complete four projects in a two-week span, divide $10,000 (your month's goal) by four (the number of projects). In this example, you'd look to charge about $2,500 per client to reach your monthly goal. (I will go through the math in more detail at the end of this chapter.)

TAKE CONTROL OF YOUR BUSINESS AND LIFE

This number may be drastically different than what you're charging now. But this exercise gives you direction for how to increase your value for ideal clients—the ones willing to pay what you're worth.

When you begin reaching your monthly goal in 50 percent of your available working time, you have the luxury of pursuing other business goals. This newfound freedom allows you to focus 25 percent of your time (or one week of the month) on branding and business development. Everything you do during this week—competitive research, content marketing, social media, and email campaigns—extends the value of your service, potentially allowing you to charge an even higher rate in the future.

And the final 25 percent of your time? If you've done the proper legwork for the other 75 percent, you've earned the right to do whatever you want with it.

That's right! You have a full week a month to yourself.

Devote time to learning more about your industry so you can better serve clients. Take on more work to boost income. Or fill this last week of the month with your own creative hobbies that have nothing to do with your business. I find that pretty much any mentally or physically stimulating activity can have positive results for your business. Travel, take dance classes, learn to surf—whatever makes you happy. When you build a Badass Brand, you have freedom, flexibility, and control over how you spend your time.

IF YOU ARE FAR FROM YOUR TARGET NUMBER...

Don't panic. If the math tells you that your target number per project is drastically higher than what you are charging now, that's great; you need this information in order to set yourself on the right path.

Let go of the desperation mindset—that you will take on any project and charge whatever you can get. Instead, seize control of the situation, and be the expert I know you are. Ask yourself these questions:

1. How can I increase the value of what I offer?

Maybe you add related services or valuable deliverables, increase your knowledge so you are even more expert at what you do, or both. In the beginning we increased the size of the websites and amount of collateral we would deliver in one day by preparing more on the front end, which allowed us to increase our prices. Then, after building up our own knowledge by marketing our own business, we added marketing consulting to our deliverables, which increased the value of the Brandup further.

2. How can I decrease the time I spend on each project without decreasing the value I provide?

If you do some of the same work for each client, you might be able to template some of it—or template 75 percent. Reevaluate your process and cut out unnecessary steps. As I mentioned earlier, we designed a bunch of templates using InDesign for social media, business cards, and other collateral that we use in every Brandup so we didn't have to remake them each time. I templated my contracts and began using Echosign to send them, instead referring to the Brandshrink Brief as the detailed SOW (Statement of Work) specific to the client. This eliminated the hour I used to spend customizing each contract. You might also, for example, move some meetings online to save yourself travel time.

It's really as straightforward as that: increase the value, decrease the time, and, of course, communicate your Badass Brand message as described in the previous chapters of this book—and you will be able to raise your prices.

Once you hit your target pricing and experience the steady flow of ideal clients, you can start raising your price. Everything else you make will be a profit bump for you! And that's when life gets really free.

CASE STUDY: PAIGE, VIDEOGRAPHER

I met Paige years ago, when she was just starting her video company. After just a few minutes speaking to this woman—who was beaming with positive energy and creativity—we realized that behind the smile lay a fiercely determined business leader.

I liked her attitude and her clear obsession with quality, so when it came time to hire a videographer for a marketing video, she was a standout in my network. (I know a ton of video companies run by great people, many of whom are friends, so this means a lot.)

My experience with Paige was flawless. She had a clear process that made us feel well taken care of. She delivered as promised, and the final product was impressive. And the price was really good.

The simple fact of working with someone with a clear and distinct process—where things happened on time and as promised, and where the final product was what we hoped for and more—is not a common experience in the small business world. I've hired many contractors and small companies for various jobs over the years, and rarely does everything go the way they say it will. This used to annoy me, but now I have a different perspective. I'm excited, because it means the bar is lower than I thought, and it's pretty easy to surpass the average competitors just by doing the minimum job required: set expectations and then meet them (yes, we want to underpromise and overdeliver; but you'd be surprised how few companies can even just deliver as promised).

A couple of months after working with Paige, she hired us for a Brandshrink. And I was amazed by what I learned.

This dynamite video company was in the position everyone else seems to be in—always hunting for clients, never sure where the next one was coming from. And she was in the perfect position to use the 50/25/25 formula.

First, I asked what she needed to be successful—by her own definition. She said $10,000 per month and time to travel.

Depending on who you are, $10,000 per month can sound like a lot or like nothing. But using the formula—and because I knew her product was well above average—I knew she could get there pretty easily if she just structured her time and process a little differently.

Each step of her video process was basically the same, and took the same amount of time. From engagement to finished video, our project lasted about six weeks. But when I questioned Paige about what she actually spent her time doing during that month-and-a-half, I found out that she lost most of it to lack of planning. The work itself didn't take six weeks.

Her steps:

1. Onboarding questionnaire—sent online
2. Story outline—delivered by her
3. Storyboard—delivered by her
4. Feedback received—from client
5. Storyboard edits—delivered by her
6. Final storyboard agreed upon—everyone
7. Shoot date 10 a.m.–6 p.m.—everyone
8. Rough cut—delivered by her
9. Feedback received—from client
10. Edits—delivered by her
11. Feedback received—from client
12. Final video—delivered by her

Feedback is a necessary part of creative projects, but a common pitfall on projects involving this step occurs when the feedback isn't defined. And Paige had this problem. She sent each round of work (see steps 3, 8 and 10) with an open-ended request for feedback.

This meant she relied on the client to get back to her in a timely manner—which never happens. I certainly didn't get back to her quickly, when I was her client! I didn't have a deadline, and I was busy doing other things. She didn't force me to make it a priority, and that meant that I put it off.

I proposed that because her process is the same each time, she schedule in all the steps, not just her steps. Make this a tight two-week process, and then use the fact that you can deliver such a Badass project in a short amount of time as a reason to charge more.

Example schedule:

- Monday Day 1: Onboarding questionnaire given live
- Monday Day 1: Story outline written
- Wednesday Day 3: Story outline delivered in morning, with scheduled call to go over feedback that afternoon
- Wednesday Day 3: Storyboard drawn
- Thursday Day 4: Storyboard delivered in morning, with scheduled call to go over feedback that afternoon
- Friday Day 5: Final storyboard delivered for approval, with tentatively scheduled call to go over feedback that afternoon
- Tuesday Day 9: SHOOT DAY (one video shoot

per week)
- Tuesday Day 9 night: Edit rough cut
- Wednesday Day 10: Deliver rough cut, with scheduled call to go over feedback that morning
- Wednesday Day 10: Make edits in afternoon
- Thursday Day 11: Deliver edited video, with scheduled call to go over feedback that afternoon
- Thursday Day 11: Make edits, finalize video
- Friday Day 12: Deliver final video

As you can see from this schedule, Tuesdays are shoot days. But Paige can spend every other day of the week working on multiple projects, because most tasks take only one to four hours.

From beginning to end, this project is done in 12 days, but Paige can think of each week as hosting one project—because only one shoot can happen per week.

If we go back to the formula, she can do four projects a month working full time. So to start she would need to sell four of these each month to make her $10,000 per month. We paid more than that and felt like we got a steal, so it's definitely doable. We can see her transition into three projects per month at $3,333—not much more than we paid and definitely doable given that she is not only delivering a great product, but also providing it quickly.

The goal to hit the 50/25/25 mark is $5,000 per project, because that would deliver her $10,000 per month with only two shoots per month, effectively giving her the equivalent of two weeks per month to do business development, build her brand, do more work and make $15,000 or $20,000 in a month, or just hang out.

If Paige finds that her clients are willing to spend $3,333 per video but $5,000 is a stretch, she can do two things: (1) look for ways to add value to the project, or (2) look for ways to decrease the time she spends on each video. One way to increase the value might be to add in a few marketing clips. Instead of just the brand video, she could make a couple of Facebook shorts that the client can use in advertising. This might cost a few more hours of time, but the increase of almost $1,700 in revenue will cover that five-fold.

THIS IS FREEDOM

Having a defined, concrete goal makes very clear what you need to sell and how much time you need to spend (or not spend) to achieve freedom. And while struggling to find clients is daunting, charging $5,000 per project won't be a big leap for Paige. When she is able to deliver in 12 days, and tightens her process so she eliminates dead time waiting for feedback from clients, she will become known for her very specific process and pricing, and the clients will come to her.

Plus, she'll have the freedom to do whatever she wants, and that's travel. She said a perfect trip would be backpacking around Thailand and Vietnam. My advice would be to take as many projects as she can, do a couple of $15,000–$20,000 months, and then go away for a couple of months. Why not?!

SHAKE YOUR BADASS

Take a good hard look at your finances. I know; it's not your favorite thing to do, but you can't price yourself for freedom if you don't know where you are and where you need to go.

1.   **Baseline Revenue Goal:** How much do you need each month to live in relative comfort? I'm not talking super luxury, but I don't mean bare bones either. Come up with a monthly dollar amount.

2.   **Cushy Revenue Goal:** How much money do you want to make each month? This number exists on the higher end of comfort.

   a. You can also have your jet/three houses/high-luxury number, but this isn't that. This is the number that you would be really happy with without becoming a millionaire. The jet is also possible for you, but usually not just by selling your services without either translating them into a scalable product or hiring employees to scale.

   b. This book doesn't teach you how to scale, but it does help create the foundation for scaling in the future. If you want to build a large organization now, I recommend reading *The E-Myth* by Michael Gerber. If you want to scale with a product, read Timothy Ferriss'

The 4-Hour Workweek—or wait for my next book about turning your Badass Brand into a scalable online course.

3.   Identify how many clients you can fully service in a 40-hour workweek with your Bull's Eye product. If your company doesn't lend itself to a Bull's Eye product, use the most common, profitable service you have. Also, condense the hours. You may work with someone for an hour a week for 10 weeks. This would allow you to service the equivalent of four clients in one week (10 hours per client multiplied by four clients equals a 40-hour workweek).

4.   Plug these numbers into the formula to see what prices you need to charge for:

a. your **Baseline Revenue Goal** in four weeks, three weeks, two weeks, and one week;

b. your **Cushy Revenue Goal** in four weeks, three weeks, two weeks, and one week.

5.   Assess where you are now in relation to these numbers. Brainstorm ways to increase the value of what you offer in order to steadily raise prices to move toward your goal revenue numbers.

FORMULA (Time to bust out that middle-school algebra!)

Revenue: **$MONEY per month**

Time per client: ***Y hours***

How to find the 50/25/25 Rule to Profit & Freedom:

80/Y hours** = **#CLIENTS per month

(*80 hours represents 2 weeks of work, or 50% of your time*)

$MONEY per month / #CLIENTS per Month = ***Price For Freedom***

Example: Mike needs $8,000 per month to live comfortably, and wants $30,000 to live a luxurious lifestyle. He does marketing packages for small businesses, each of which takes 30 hours of his time.

Baseline Revenue Goal: $8,000 per month

Cushy Revenue Goal: $30,000 per month

Time per client: 30 hours

First Revenue goal: **$MONEY per month= $8,000**

Time per client: ***30 hours***

How to find the 50/25/25 Rule to Profit & Freedom:

80/30 hours** = **#CLIENTS/Month = 2.67

$MONEY per month / #CLIENTS per Month = ***Price For Freedom***

$8,000 / 2.67 = $3,000

At $3,000 per client Mike would be able to spend 50 percent of this time working directly with clients making $8,000 per month, giving him 25 percent of his time to work on brand building and 25 percent of his time to use as he pleases.

Mike's prices may be a far cry from $3,000 per client, so at first he will aim for working with clients 75 percent of the time. Instead of using 80 hours we'll use 120 hours (3 weeks of work instead of 2), so 120/30 = 4 clients, and $8,000/4 clients = $2,000/client (working 3 weeks a month).

Once he accomplishes this and has a full docket, Mike's next goal to achieve the 50/25/25 Rule is to move from four clients per month to an average of 2.66 clients/month, charging $3,000/client.

This simplifies everything for Mike. His goal is an average of 2.66 clients each month (32 clients a year), each of which pays $3,000 a project—and he must make sure he does not spend more than 30 hours per project. Once he's achieved this, he can continue to increase the value of his brand and business to steadily increase his prices and profits. And work toward his **Cushy Revenue Goal:** 2.66 clients/month charging $11,252/client—which will mean he achieved the

50/25/25 Rule making $30,000/month!

While that might seem outlandish for Mike—who may not even be charging $1,500 per project right now—remember: this is a process. If Mike continues to deliver this process, learn and improve upon it, and steadily increase the value of his projects and his brand—by investing time or money in education, creating content and building reputation, all the while increasing the value of his offering and/or decreasing the amount of time spent—then $11,252 is not as far off as it seems. It took us less than a year to go from $2,950 days to $9,950 days, and we got there by setting a goal and working toward it, instead of just increasing the price as much as we could.

WHAT LIVING WITHOUT ELECTRICITY ON AN ISLAND TAUGHT ME ABOUT BADASS BRANDING

Steve and I didn't follow the typical path to starting a business, and we didn't start out with the intention of building a brand. As I mentioned, we just wanted to work for ourselves; if we could support ourselves without reporting to a boss, we would be happy.

And unlike most business owners I meet, we had the benefit of starting with nothing to lose. You see, the seed was planted in a very unlikely place—while we were literally planting seeds on an organic farm in the

Caribbean.

Back in 2011, Steve and I decided to retire early. Really early. At ages 31 and 27, respectively. With a total of $10,000 in our savings account, we sublet our Brooklyn apartment and bought one-way tickets to Tortola in the British Virgin Islands. We hooked up with a farm through WWOOF.org (Willing Workers On Organic Farms) that allowed us to trade manual labor for the opportunity to live and eat off the land, allowing us to experience the simple life with virtually no money.

We lived without clocks, phones, computers, or internet access for three months, building fires to cook all our meals. We slept according to the sun and, because we had no clock, can only guess that we would wake up around 4 or 5 a.m. with the roosters, and work until about 9 or 10 that morning.

After that, the day was ours. We usually walked or hitchhiked to one of the many idyllic beaches to swim and read. We inhaled books; first the stack of classics we brought by Hess, Rushdie, and Coelho, and then whatever we could swap with other WWOFers and nomads we met.

We got used to being mistaken for college students. We had a memorable conversation with an older couple we met at Buzzards Bay Beach, who got a little snippy with us:

Woman: "You kids on vacation?"

Me: "Nope, we decided to retire early and live the good life now!"

Man: "That's not how it works. You've got to put your time in first, work hard, build your career, so when you retire, you earned it."

Steve: "But why would we do all that when we can just come down here now?"

Woman: "You kids are all the same. You don't want to work. You want to just lay on the beach and have things handed to you."

In truth, we weren't looking to avoid work at all. We were just exploring our options. We wanted to see if island life—free of money (we bartered for most things), stress, and to-do lists—was for us. We wanted to experience the life that so many people, ourselves included, hold up on a pedestal as what they would do if only they didn't have to worry about money.

Except we didn't want to wait until we had a ton of money to do it! Sure, we weren't living a luxurious lifestyle (did I mention we had to make fires for all our meals?), but we didn't care; we were in paradise!

However, the bubble popped early in our trip and we learned a profound lesson: Life is life, wherever you are. The people we met in Tortola had similar problems and similar stresses to people in New York. We realized that how we look at life and approach it, no matter where we are, is going to create the life we ultimately experience. The environment is secondary.

So we thought maybe we could live the island life in Brooklyn!

With a lot of time to think and talk, we designed the life we wanted. We always knew we wanted to work for ourselves, and given that we had gotten used to living on almost nothing, this was the best time to jump off that cliff.

We decided that we weren't going to look for jobs when we returned to Brooklyn. Instead, I would find freelance work for Steve and manage the clients, and he would do the creative part. Going home to New York City four months later with only $3,000 meant there was no room for failure; we had to make it work.

(I realize there is a one-month discrepancy in there. In one last-ditch effort to explore different lifestyles, we spent the fourth month of our trip crewing on a sailboat, sailing around the West Indies. Was living on a sailboat the life for us, we wondered? It was fun, but no!)

The first year was a hustle, but we had a huge advantage. We started our business after spending four months living without electricity. We were used to surviving off beans and rice and showering with a jug of cold water.

When the bar is set so low, practically everything in Brooklyn is luxurious living. Big comfy bed with no mosquitos? Sweet! Long, hot showers where you actually feel clean at the end? Amazing! Chicken wings? *Have we died and gone to heaven*?!?!

We were easy to please.

This meant we didn't need to make a lot to sustain ourselves. Just being able to live and work together, and pay for it, was an exciting prospect.

Had I known then what I know now, I could have used the 50/25/25 formula to identify exactly how much we needed to charge to achieve the freedom we were looking for in Tortola. At first, we were living off about $3,000 per month by eating only rice, beans, and veggies. If we could have developed our $3,000 per day Brandup back then, we could have worked one day a month and had the rest of the month to ourselves!

Talk about freedom.

**"Not so fast,
I've got a few questions for you..."**

CHAPTER SIX

THE MOST IMPORTANT WORD IN BUSINESS: NO

One of the best business-development lessons we ever learned was to turn down business.

When we began Worstofall Design, we were looking for clients—any clients. We said yes to anyone willing to pay because we needed the money—and also, why the hell not?

What I didn't understand was that saying yes to anyone willing to pay was killing us.

BLAND ISN'T A FLAVOR

By accepting everything that came our way, we were keeping our agency generic and stifling our ability to grow our brand's reputation.

Even when we were doing okay during those first

three years, I was in a constant state of heightened anxiety.

Where would our next clients come from? When would we land them? Would we earn enough to live? It was an unremitting struggle to keep that pipeline full.

Only when we further developed our brand, found our place, and started turning away clients did our company truly begin to thrive. The more we said no to those outside of our specific niche, the more clients we got. And these weren't just any kind of clients; they were the ideal people we wanted to work with. They wanted to hire us for exactly what we did best, and were willing to pay a premium to work with us.

NICE IN THEORY...

Sure, saying no sounds great in theory. But in the real world, this may be nearly impossible. How do you say no to a client when you need money—especially when you are capable of doing what they are requesting?

You do it when you understand that not all dollars are equal.

Back in the summer of 2015, we didn't understand that. Even though we had narrowed our offering and were doing strictly Brandups for about nine months—steadily raising our prices each month, yet always filling our calendar with clients—we still got sucked in by the enticement of money.

One day, a potential client called requesting a new brand for his e-commerce website.

Potential client: Found your site, love your work. I think you guys are perfect for us because we need this site up and running as soon as possible.

Me: How soon?

Potential Client: Wish we had it yesterday. So ideally in the next two weeks.

Me: Well, technically we can do that, and I don't know any other companies that can do this type of work in two weeks! But we don't really deal with e-commerce or products. We focus on brand strategy and website design for service businesses. And we don't build ecommerce websites, or work with Wordpress.

Potential Client: What if you just made the designs, and we had our guys implement them on Wordpress? Then all we need is the brand and the homepage design.

Me: So the brand and homepage design, in the next two weeks, for $10,000. Usually I don't think it makes sense for people to pay us that much without getting the actual website.

Potential Client: Can you please make an exception? We need this done now, and we love your style. We've had so many bad experiences with designers, and they *all take forever. We would be happy to pay $10,000 for you to get it done because we trust you.*

Well, technically we could do it. We are always booked solid, but we also leave a week open for internal and personal projects, and that week happened to be coming up. The flattery didn't hurt! For $10,000, I could make an exception.

So we agreed and executed the Brandshrink brief. We learned that the client's business was delivering brand-name goods to Africa from all over the world at affordable prices. Their mission was smart, and their model made sense. But what separated them from other companies like this? There were many details to explain—and the challenge was that the client wanted to include so many details that we didn't know how to rein them in.

But there was a bigger problem: This was not our specialty. We know small service businesses like the back of our hands. Not only have we successfully built one ourselves, but we've also worked with hundreds and can confidently say what will and won't work.

Large e-commerce delivery services on another continent, though? We know nothing about that. No idea how to sell things in Africa, and definitely not experts in e-commerce.

The situation was becoming clear: We had a client who wanted to work with us, but we were totally out of our element.

We started to realize this Brandup wasn't setting us, or this client, up for success.

FACE A SHITTY SITUATION HEAD-ON

We continued to prepare anyway because of the tight timeline, and we made some great-looking designs that were in line with what the client had requested. But when Steve and I walked to the client's office early to start the first day, we were both dreading the project.

We were going to charge them our fee to do something we didn't believe in. We knew they would be happy with it because they liked our work, and our design would completely change their company's look. But we couldn't stand firmly behind any design decisions because we didn't have enough authority in the space, so we were essentially going to be acting as the hands to execute their vision. Even if they were ultimately going to be happy, we didn't think they should be paying a premium rate for this, and we didn't want to do it. If all they wanted was a designer to make something that looked nice, they had much cheaper options.

So we turned down $10,000 the morning of a project,

even though we had completed all the prep work and could have easily done it and made them happy.

It was the best no we ever said.

SAY NO WITH INTEGRITY

Of course, Steve and I called the client and apologized. I explained why we had to back out: I didn't feel comfortable charging them our high fee for the work we were going to do. I said we would give them all the prep work anyway, and that they could have the awesome designs and find someone cheap to implement them. They got some great design work without having to pay, and I hoped it would make up for us canceling at the last minute.

They understood, and there were no hard feelings. They were happy to receive the designs for free, and Steve and I danced down the street, excited to escape a nightmare couple of days.

STAYING TRUE TO OUR VALUE HAD LONG-LASTING LESSONS

This experience solidified our stance as a company that did work only for service businesses. We knew we wouldn't even entertain products because it just wasn't worth it. There are plenty of service businesses in need of our Brandups, and we know we can crush it every time. The value of what we are selling is highest for those types of clients, so that's all we want to do.

And that's the main point of saying no in the first place: to create time for the clients you love—to work with the clients for whom you can do your best.

LESSON #6: THE POWER OF NO

The opportunity cost of spending time with the wrong client is enough to justify a solid commitment to finding only the right kind of people to work with. Working with only your ideal clients has exponential benefits:

- Ideal clients help you build your reputation in your ideal niche.
- Those who you enjoy working with become great case studies to share with future clients, as well as amazing referral sources.
- Ideal clients help you learn more about your process, in turn helping you apply what you've learned to the next project. Each client brings unique challenges—and the more of them you overcome, the more nuanced expertise you can bring to the table.
- Each project helps you refine your process, therefore increasing the value (and price) and decreasing the time spent on it. You are

continually sharpening your process and becoming more efficient.

- Finally, you increase your profit! If you aren't making profit, you'll soon find yourself with an entire new set of issues to stress about.

IDEAL CLIENTS INCREASE YOUR VALUE EXPONENTIALLY

Money from an ideal client increases your credibility in the market in your area of expertise, as each successful project produces another referral. Each meaningful project is another opportunity to increase your value and therefore your future pricing model.

But when you work with clients outside your niche, all you are doing is making money. You're not getting the added benefits listed above. In essence, you are losing value in your business. It might seem as though a paying client is better than no client. But when you're working with them, you're forced to spend time away from finding—or servicing—other appropriate clients. You're missing out on projects that are better suited for you, and it's never worth it.

ARE YOU READY TO SAY NO?

It might seem like a pretty simple question after I've laid out all the reasons for doing so. However, it can feel extremely difficult when you come face to face with it in the real world. In fact, most people can't stick to it.

Let's say you're a marketing consultant for the financial industry, and someone wants to hire you to do marketing for their pet store. You have the skills, so you could technically do it—and you need the money. So why not?

Or someone wants to buy your $5,000 VIP consulting day, but wants to pay only $4,000 for it.

Or someone wants to hire you to cater their 10-person dinner party, but you usually prefer large parties because they command a much higher price for only slightly more work.

Saying no to a client offering you money in the real world is really hard, and most people think by doing so you are leaving money on the table.

WHEN TURNING DOWN WORK ACTUALLY *INCREASES* YOUR BOTTOM LINE

Essentially, a dollar today from a client outside your niche is worth less than a dollar tomorrow from an ideal client. The dollar you receive today is only cash. But when you work with someone who fits into your target demographic, you receive additional payments in the following ways:

• Saying no strengthens your message. Those who want to hire you but don't fit into your business model just got a great lesson in your specialization. If you focus on small businesses and turn down a corporate client, that person will think of you the next time a small-business friend needs your services. You have just created a wonderful referral source of someone who understands exactly what you sell and is more likely to remember you for it.

• Nobody forgets the company that said no. They remember the company that had enough understanding of their own value to pass up instant equity.

• Saying no frees you up to find new clients who will help you build and strengthen your business into the kind of company you want it to be. People tend to surround themselves with those similar to them, and clients beget more clients like them. If you discount your service or agree to complete a project you don't enjoy or that falls outside your niche, those clients will only be a referral source for other similar jobs—the kind you don't want.

Imagine if you only worked with your favorite, most profitable clients, the ones who fill your day with delight. The ones that respect your work and pay you on time. Clients who think you are incredible because of how much value you bring to them. The ones who are easiest to work with because they fall into your specialty.

Don't you want a business where all your clients are ideal clients? You can have it if you just learn to say NO.

Badass Brands don't say yes to everyone.

So—are you ready to say no?

This is not a quick or one-time decision. You'll have to answer this question over and over. But the more you practice saying no, the more value you will see from it, and the better you'll get at doing it.

HERE ARE IMPORTANT TIMES TO SAY NO:
It's important to say no when...friends and family ask for work

Let's face it: Friends and family are the worst clients. Even when they are paying you, they (and you) feel that you owe them more than other clients. And they're usually needier because of your personal relationship. This isn't meant to knock your friends or family, it's just the nature of the situation. It's very hard to keep the relationship professional, which means you end up giving a lot.

I avoid any kind of paid so-called favor work at all costs. However, that doesn't mean you can't be helpful; in fact, it's quite the opposite. When it makes sense we've given friends and family advice and we've even designed small things for them for free because we love them and we want to help. But I prefer not to enter into a professional relationship because it can get messy. I'd rather find other clients where I can dictate the terms from the beginning and keep it profitable. Those casual texts and phone calls really add up! Once they pay, we often feel we have no right to be too busy for them. That's when they expect you to drop everything to help them at any moment because they're your client AND your friend.

Don't do it. Your business will suffer.

It's important to say no when...you are asked to lower your price

We've all been here. It can feel disheartening, frustrating, and sometimes offensive when prospects ask you to discount your services. And all those feelings usually result in an uncomfortable and often counterproductive reaction. When you are clear on the value you provide and believe in the prices you charge, it is much easier to respond to these bargain-hunters.

There are two common situations where this might happen:

1. You write a proposal after collecting all the

information, and the client comes back asking for a lower price.

2.   You have standard prices and someone asks you for a discount.

Post-proposal discount requests can be infuriating. After investing time and effort into pitching the client, now you have to weigh the prospect of losing the client or taking a pay cut. You can feel cornered, especially when you need clients.

Requests for discounts on preset pricing happen less frequently, which is another solid argument for productizing your most popular services. If someone ever does ask for a discount off a package, a simple "no" is sufficient (although a hearty laugh in the face is sometimes warranted).

Discount seekers aren't necessarily bad people; some individuals believe asking for a discount is a smart business practice. Maybe they are just starting out and don't have a lot of money, and they are hoping you can relate. Some people think that being a friend or a friend of a friend means you'll be willing to give them a deal.

However, when you give in to a discount, you're essentially telling the client that your price was arbitrary, that you don't value your own work, and that maybe others don't either. After all, if you had other clients knocking on your door to pay full price you would never entertain the idea of discounting your services! The subliminal message is that you are trying to get more money out of them than you need or believe your service is worth. Give in to their request, and you give the client control of the project—and the relationship. And that never ends well.

You can view a request for a discount as your opportunity to show them just how valuable you are. Tell them this is not an arbitrary number; the price represents the value of the service. Remember that if they don't pay your price, someone else will, and you would actually be losing money by taking them on as a client at a discount. Your high-paying client might be right around the corner—and if you take on this project, you'll be too busy to see them.

In the event that a client genuinely doesn't have the money to meet your price, another way you can give them a deal is to take something away. They want to hire you to write all their website copy but want a discount? Allow only one round of edits instead of the usual three (or no edits, depending on the discount). By meeting their price but taking something away from your deliverables, you show that your price has valid reasoning behind it. You retain control of the situation, keep their respect, and still allow them to pay the price they can afford to get something of value from you. It's a win-win.

It's important to say no when...prospects question your brand or business

Be your brand—unapologetically. Badass Brands don't apologize for who they are and what they stand for; they relish it. Every time someone doesn't get their brand, every time someone is confused by what they are saying or doesn't like how they say it, every time Great-Aunt Nancy gives advice on how they really should be selling their services, Badass Brands smile to themselves, knowing the naysayers are just not their clients.

When you draw a line in the sand and own your brand, you are actually saying no to everyone except your ideal target demographic. By having a strong personality—and standing against something that others actually like—you are saying no to everyone else.

Take Stash Wealth as an example. Their competitors are buttoned up and corporate. Many people looking for financial help want their advisor to wear a suit and tie and work on Wall Street. These people won't like Stash's sassy voice and Brooklyn-style attire; they may think ripped jeans (even designer ones) and a blazer is unprofessional.

By being their brand Stash is saying no to these clients. When corporate types tell them they should dress differently or communicate differently on their website, they say no every time they ignore that advice. And they do it because their ideal clients love their walk and talk. They attract the exact clientele they want to work with, and they are okay repelling the rest.

It can be hard in the beginning; after all, it's human nature to want to be liked. But over time, as you experience love from your people and your fans, you'll view everyone who dislikes what you say as a representation of your brand's strength. After all, if it wasn't powerful, it wouldn't evoke that kind of response. It's arguably a major reason your business is going places, so soak it up.

It's important to say no when...requests for work fall outside your Badass niche

You need money, you have the capabilities, and someone wants to pay you to do something that's not exactly what you do. But it's related, so why not do it?

Every time you put energy into something outside your specialty, you are taking time away from building your brand and expertise. Every time you do something new you are reinventing the wheel. It may require coming up with a new process, writing a new contract, and making mistakes. It will almost certainly cost you more time than anticipated. This not only eats into your profits, but it also has no added benefit for the brand you are building. It's just cash in hand, and usually unprofitable cash at that. The case study later in this chapter brings this idea to life.

To recap, no is the most valuable word in business because:

1. It strengthens your brand in the eyes of all prospects and potential referral sources. Nobody likes hearing no, but they definitely remember it. And then they remember you and your expertise, which is the ultimate goal of a branding. If you can achieve this while avoiding a pain-in-the-ass, unprofitable client, DO IT.

2. Clients who are not the perfect fit will become an excellent referral source. I've gotten some of my best referrals from prospects that didn't work out. A law firm we turned down because there were too many opinions involved in the project sent us a perfect client a few weeks later—the friend of one of the partners had a small firm that needed rebranding. By turning down the big firm we really articulated who we were for, and that smaller project was ideal for us.

3.   Saying no to unprofitable work now frees you

up to find better, more profitable clients for the future. These clients are easier to work with and willing to pay more for your expertise—with the added benefit of building your brand and reputation for the future.

4. It shows integrity in what you do, and that makes you more referable. Nobody likes being sold to, and I don't send referrals to anyone who is a hard sell because it reflects poorly on me. When I make a referral, I take care to send only people with the integrity to say no to a project that isn't right for them. On the flip side, I send anyone and everyone to my contacts who have integrity and won't take a project that isn't right. Even if I'm not clear if they are a good fit, I'm happy to make the introduction because I trust they will point my referral in a different direction, if necessary.

LIKE MOST PEOPLE, YOU MIGHT BE SCARED RIGHT NOW

There is an inevitable gap between creating a more focused business model and achieving a healthy revenue stream. I get the following question a lot: What happens between when you focus your business and when the money starts rolling in?

The fear of this gap in income is the reason we call it a BADASS brand. Not a good brand or a great brand. A BADASS brand that requires you to stare fear in the face and laugh.

Most people can't handle the fear.

You see, it's a dark, scary place you have to pass through first—turning down customers and, therefore, money.

How do you make this jump in a practical way?

You need to make money, and many of your contacts may still think of you as an all-things-to-all-people brand. So how should you market yourself during this crucial time period?

There's no easy way around it: You need to trust yourself.

Trust that the fear you experience is the canyon between who you are now and the invincible Badass you will become—and that it is worth it.

The side you're on now is the Everything-to-Everyone Cliff. The other side is the Badass Brand Mountaintop. If you want to reach it, you'll have to take the leap. And there's no question that there will be a lull.

But how long will that dip be, and what should you do in the meantime?

The length of that lull depends on (1) the effort you put into educating the world on your niche, (2) your prices, and (3) your confidence level. Passively hoping clients will find you is not productive. Instead, attend a networking meeting every morning for a month and call everyone on your contact list to update them. If you do this intensively for one month, you will never have to do it again.

Hit the ground running with a clear target and message, and success will come very quickly. When we decided to do only Brandups and say no to all other work, I called old prospects to whom I had submitted proposals for large projects. I told them our offer no longer stood—we had changed our model, and we could now do the same project but in two days and at a fraction of the cost. Three signed up on the spot. But it required some legwork on my part.

I often say that a Badass Brand allows you to attract clients instead of chasing them, and I mean it. But you have to plant the seeds! This takes upfront work. And that work garners bigger and better results when you are clear about what you offer—and then further strengthen your brand's positioning in the world every time you say no.

So am I saying that you need to pick a niche and never waver?

On the one hand, I think you must commit to your niche 100 percent for it to succeed. However, if someone asks for something outside your specialty and you need the cash, who am I to say you can't?

Especially if it's not too far outside and it's not going to drain all your energy. Of course you can, but be aware it's going to prolong the good stuff because it will take focus away from your target.

A consulting company we worked with, Yeh Ideology, pivoted its business to focus on large corporate clients looking to hire top-tier innovation team members. But while they were making the pivot they were getting lots of inquiries from job-seekers looking for high-level consulting advice—and willing to pay $500 an hour for it. Pivoting can create a gap in income, so it made perfect sense to work with these clients because Yeh already had the expertise and infrastructure to accommodate them. While it might have slightly prolonged the ramp-up of corporate clients by diverting their attention, they had more overhead and needed the cash to keep their team in place during the transition.

You know your situation and what's best for you. But there is always room to be gutsier than you are comfortable with. My advice? Be the Badass I know you are! Jump off the cliff and grow wings on the way down. Just *how good are you*? How much do you believe in your abilities? How much value are you really bringing to the table? How committed are you to becoming more and more Badass at your expertise with everything that you do? How committed are you to learning and growing?

If you're desperate for money, do what you need to do. But the quickest way to get your brand where you want it to be is to stay the course.

CASE STUDY: RUSSELL, WEDDING PHOTOGRAPHER

Russell is a wedding photographer who generally shoots on the weekends. Although there is a great deal of post-wedding work, his weekdays are fairly flexible. So when his friend Tom's girlfriend Sally asks if he can do some headshots for her LinkedIn profile, he says yes. He could use the extra income.

He thinks headshots are easy and can probably be done in an hour, with another hour for selecting and editing. He charges $5,000 for weddings, so he'll charge $300 dollars for this project, a decent and fair rate.

Sally shows up to the shoot with a pile of clothes. She has no idea which outfit to wear. She asks if it's okay to take photos in a few different looks.

No problem, Russell thinks. But once the shoot gets rolling and she's on her third outfit, he realizes this is going to take longer than expected. He didn't know outfit changes were going to take up so much time. Plus, she did her own hair and makeup, and it's not looking right in the photos. Russell doesn't know how to do makeup and hair because his brides always have it done professionally. When he looks at the shots, he knows immediately that the lighting is washing her out. He tells her to put on more makeup, which also takes time.

The shoot ends up being two hours. Russell was an hour off, but he's still going to take home $300 he wouldn't have made otherwise. He could have just been watching TV during that time, so what's an hour?

The next day he looks through the shots. Because of the makeup debacle, only half are even usable. He finally finds a few good ones, picks his top five, and sends them to Sally. She writes back immediately. The ones he sent are not what she had in mind; she wants images where she looks more professional. Sally thinks she looks too friendly.

Too friendly is not how Russell is feeling right now. He goes through the photos again and finds some that could be considered more professional. Sally replies that these are better, but she wants to take a look through all of the images and choose herself.

Frustration has now turned into annoyance. Russell has already spent almost an hour sifting through the photos and doesn't want to lose any more time on this project. But he doesn't feel like he has a choice. Sally clearly doesn't like what he has picked, and he just wants her to choose the photos so he can move on to editing them.

Sally picks a couple of photos, but her hair looks weird. She asks if Russell can Photoshop her hair from a different picture onto her face. This will take even more time. But Sally has made it clear that she doesn't like any of the other photos, and Russell doesn't want to upset her. After all, he has bent over backward so far and would hate to spend all this time and still send away an unhappy client.

So he does the work. After another hour he has produced the photo she wants. He sends it off, relieved that it's over, and psyched to spend the $300 on some well-deserved beers.

But like a zombie, Sally keeps coming back. She is pleased with this image, but didn't he say he would provide three final shots? Unfortunately, unlike a zombie, Russell's brain is still in working order, and he has to continue to deal with this so-called side project.

And on and on it goes. If you think this is an exaggeration, you've never worked with clients. The thing is, it's not Sally's fault. This happened because Russell had no process.

If Russell regularly did headshots, he would have given Sally instructions ahead of time. He would have recommended hiring a makeup artist for an additional fee (even better, he would have included it in the price). He would let her know she was allowed up to three changes of clothes. He would have asked her ahead of time to show him some examples of photos she liked and wanted to emulate. This way, when he picked the top five photos, he would know that they were in line with what she wanted (and if she didn't like them, he would have been able to refer to a concrete example). He would have specified that his services included only one round of editing, and that any additional rounds or extreme editing—like Photoshopping two photos together—would cost extra.

But this is not something Russell does every day, so he doesn't have a process for it—which means he doesn't yet have a way of making it profitable. It wouldn't have been lucrative if he had developed that process just for Sally, as he would have spent that extra time developing the process. Unless Russell wants to add headshots to his repertoire, he needs to say no to customers looking for work outside his niche of weddings.

Imagine if he had spent that same four to five hours working to land another $5,000 wedding client instead. That marketing work may have even planted the seeds for a few additional wedding clients. The value of his time spent is incomparable!

Plus, he didn't even receive the value of more potential business—the last thing he wants is for one of Sally's friends to contact him for more LinkedIn headshots! Sally is unlikely to give him a referral for weddings because that's not why she hired him. He's not top of mind for weddings for her; if anything, he's top of mind for headshots.

Not all dollars are equal, and staying in your niche means exponential dollars in the future. Your time is better spent getting ideal clients over and over, the ones for whom you have a tried-and-true process that will only become more refined over time.

When you spread yourself thin trying to do work for everyone who asks, you'll be stuck on a hamster wheel looking for clients. And that will drive you crazy.

SHAKE YOUR BADASS

- Make a list of current clients you wouldn't say yes to again, and specify why.
- Imagine saying no to these clients. Be polite and use the conversation as a way to educate them on your specialty. This conversation is turning them into amazing referral sources, so it's just as important as speaking to a potential client.
- Practice, practice, practice your pitch, explaining your specialty and your value—and, if you have it, your lead product. This is the most important conversation you will have over and over again, and odds are you're going to stumble the first few—or even many—times. But with practice it will become second nature and ooze confidence, and that's Badass.
- Define your parameters: When will you say no to a client in terms of price, scope of work, area of expertise, or any other boundaries? To help you figure this out, visualize a situation where you don't need money. Who would you say no to in that situation? Now, how close can you get to that in the real world?
- Be honest—are you ready to say no? What's stopping you?

- Make a list of all the things in your life that are requiring you to say yes in the short term to not-so-great clients. How many can you eliminate (just for a little while)? Kids and a mortgage stay; fancy dinners out and your Zappos habit can go—remember, it's for the greater good of your business!

- Which of your current clients would you dump if you could?

- What can you do during the gap to shorten it as much as possible? Make a list of all your resources, including past clients, your network, and events. How long will it take you to reeducate them on your area of focus?

WHAT BUILDING STEVE'S ART BRAND HAS TAUGHT US ABOUT BADASS BRANDING

The value of art is arguably manufactured, which makes it a great study in the art of branding. Yes, there is value in an enjoyable piece of artwork, but that value is in the eye of the beholder. There is no intrinsic significance in a painting; that's what makes branding and marketing art particularly fascinating. It is the process of manufacturing fame, which is why the study of art is so helpful to the study of branding and marketing (although I've found that art-world people don't want to admit this).

People don't tend to think of selling their art as a business; in fact, many artists feel that "sales" and "business" are dirty words that taint art. But if you strip away this emotion, they are very similar and require similar tactics. And saying no applies just as much to art as it does to any business.

DETERMINING THE VALUE OF WORK

People have such a different relationship with art and artists than they do with almost any other product or business. Unless a gallery is showing a particular artist's work, friends often think you should give them art for free because you enjoy doing it. On the flip side, many artists feel bad for charging for their art because they think it undermines their passion.

We believe both these attitudes are a result of a manipulated art market. We built the brand #SELLOUT to shine a light on the art narrative.

When we sold art on the street, we haggled and bargained because we would rather take less cash than lug a painting home again. We had lots of time and no money.

But years later, when we had a business, the art didn't need to sell. This is the exact position you want to be in, because this is when you can hold your ground on pricing. It's also important for the value and integrity of the artist. If one person buys a painting for $2,000 and you then sell a similar piece for $1,000, the first buyer got gypped. They have a piece they like, but the price was arbitrary. How can you tell someone a piece is worth a certain amount of money when the price could decrease in the future?

We felt it was critical to set and maintain prices, and raise them with demand. They were no longer arbitrary: these were the prices we needed in order to maintain the value of the work. Similarly, if you know what your services are worth, you mustn't waver, lest you make your prices meaningless.

With some years under our belt, we can see the difference. People have bought paintings and told us that they see the prices going up, and want to make sure they get their piece before it's too expensive.

FINAL THOUGHTS

PEOPLE CAN BE SUCH BUMMERS—*YOU DO YOU*

You will never build something truly special and unique if you're not willing to be uncomfortable. You have to be able to laugh at people telling you you're doing it wrong, and instead do what you know is great and valuable.

When you're making something new, most people won't get it at first, and this can be deflating.

Here you are, with this awesome new idea that you're psyched about. Then when you excitedly tell all your people, they shake their heads and tell you why it won't work.

I know. People can be such bummers.

It's only after you become successful that the naysayers hop on board and applaud you for the genius that you are. If you're being a Badass, you may have to be a lone Badass at first (well, not totally alone; we'll be right here with you!).

Most people that come to us are like Priya from Stash Wealth. They aren't even aware that they aren't letting their true Badass come out because of an unknown fear of being different and judged.

We all have that fear. But you can't conquer it until you know you have it.

So embrace your brand and your viewpoint by acknowledging your fear and doing it anyway. This is the definition of a Badass.

NEXT STEPS

My intention for this book is to provide both high-level strategy ideas and inspiration, and tangible ways to implement those concepts. I shared our stories—both personal and professional—to show you that I'm not speaking from an ivory tower; I'm in the weeds, right alongside you. I hope to share the insights that took me years to understand so you can implement them into your business in weeks instead of years.

But you have to take action. These ideas mean nothing if you don't implement, fail, and keep trying. And you will fall on your face a few times. But if you can keep picking yourself up and following these principles, you will find the freedom you want in your life.

If you want more help, I can offer you two additional resources:

1.   Sign up to get my weekly Forbes articles at worstofalldesign.com/follow. I publish content constantly, so if you find the stories and ideas in this book motivating, follow me as I continue to learn, grow, and share additional lessons along the way.

2.   If you want to get this done right now, you can hire us to implement the brand for you. As you know, the first step is the Brandshrink! You can book one at WorstofallDesign.com/Brandshrink.

IT'S TIME TO BUILD YOUR BADASS BRAND

I've shared the tumultuous path we took to creating our Badass Brand, and numerous other stories to illustrate how Badassery can exist in any industry—and take many different forms. The insights and steps I've shared are, in our opinion, the fastest way to succeed in a small service business. Indeed, whenever I encounter a small business owner who has been struggling— sometimes for years—they are usually operating in complete contrast to the approaches described in this book.

And as long as you are a small service business, I know these methods will work for you. We've

Badassified creative companies like photographers, architects, and a poetic workshop company (true story), but we've also successfully employed these strategies for general contractors, financial advisors, and lawyers. The philosophies and strategies work for every industry if you have the guts to employ them.

But you have to say no to being a me-too brand. In fact, you have to get ready to say no to a lot of things that probably feel comfortable right now. It sounds simple, but it's not always easy.

But every time it feels hard, or you want to quit and go back to the same old way you've been doing things, remember this: If building a Badass Brand were easy, everyone would be doing it and you'd have a lot more competition.

If you picked up this book in the first place, you have what it takes, because not everyone is going to pick up a book that says "Badass" on the cover to build their business. And that's by design. We attract Badasses because they have the grit to take the hard steps necessary to get the glory.

All right, ready? LET'S DO THIS!

ABOUT THE AUTHOR

Entrepreneur, speaker and author Pia Silva is a partner and brand strategist at Worstofall Design where they build **Badass Brands without the BS**. She is a weekly Forbes contributor on branding for small businesses and has spoken at a host of entrepreneurial organizations including the Million Dollar Women Summit and Goldman Sach's 10,000 Small Businesses. Her company was named top "10 Design Firms Lead By Young People That Are Changing the Way We Look at the World" by Complex. She has a B.A. in Economics from Wesleyan University and previously attended Hunter College High School (for the 3 people who know what that is). She lives and works in Brooklyn with her husband and business partner, the brilliant artist Steve Wasterval.

Made in the USA
Lexington, KY
08 March 2018